Bolton Abbey
The Time of my Life

by

Donald Wood

Edited by **Val Rowell**

To Audrey with best wishes.

Donald Wood

Foreword by

His Grace, The Duke of Devonshire, K.G., M.C.

Dedication

I dedicate this book to Val, Elizabeth, William, Rosalind and George and especially to Joyce, with whom I spent many happy years, and finally to all those wonderful people who have played a part in giving me "the time of my life."

Cover photographs:
Front—Ferryhouse, Bolton Abbey
Back—Donald Wood

Third edition November 1996

Published in the United Kingdom in 1996

ISBN 0 9529231 0 6

Typeset in CG Triumvirate, printed and bound in the United Kingdom by Lamberts Printers, Station Road, Settle, North Yorkshire BD24 9AA

Published by Donald Wood,
Ferryhouse, Bolton Abbey, Skipton, North Yorkshire BD23 6HB

Foreword by His Grace The Duke of Devonshire, K.G., M.C.

Bolton Abbey
Skipton
Yorkshire
BD23 6AL
Bolton Abbey 260 15 August 1996

With the exception of the war years, my family and I have been visiting Bolton Abbey since my earliest recollections.

My first memory is of 1926 which was the last occasion King George V shot at Bolton Abbey. Two particular events stand out in my mind. I was then six and the pony on which I was riding from the moor bolted and I raced past the King shouting "Fire, fire, murder, murder."

The second was that I was allowed to greet the King on his return to the Hall with the news that England had beaten Australia to win The Ashes and I handed him a piece of paper with the exact scores.

I was also lucky enough to be sent on a course at Ilkley in 1941 or 42 as an anti-tank officer. There was a range on the east side of the moor. Although my own performance was extremely inaccurate, I managed to get the commander of the course a couple of days shooting and the result was a glowing report for me and some extra days leave.

My family's annual visits to Bolton Abbey are among the happiest weeks of our year.

In one way or another Bolton Abbey, its estate and moors hold nothing but the happiest of memories for me. During my life I have done a great deal of walking here and abroad, but there is nothing better than the walk from the Hall to Simon's Seat.

I am delighted to welcome this book by Donald Wood and I am sure it will prove a popular success.

Devonshire

About the Book . . .

This is a cheerful book of country life in the quieter years of the Twenties and Thirties in the picturesque Wharfedale village of Bolton Abbey. The Author describes his growing up on their small farm, his schooldays and the work of their family firm, 'Woods', based at The Smithy at Bolton Abbey, which was then the centre of village life. (The Smithy is now 'Forge Cafe' and garage). There are lively accounts of contacts with Royalty, the famous and rich people who came for the grouse shooting or were guests at the Devonshire Arms Hotel, the development at that time, of transport, from the 'packmen' who carried their own goods for sale, horse-drawn vehicles, through to the early cars and buses which have been described with detail and insight. The life experienced by the farmer and the cottager, the style of living and personalities at the Devonshire Arms Hotel and the work of the Duke of Devonshire's Bolton Abbey Estate have also been recalled with a wealth of detail and humorous anecdotes.

What a period this was! At the end of the book you will be sorry 'Woods' no longer exists since it was such a lively centre of village life and that this 'gentler' time when the pace of life was slower has also passed. However, Bolton Abbey seems to be in a 'time warp' and looks the same, and the Author still lives there.

About the Author . . .

Donald Wood, was born in Nidderdale and came to live at Bolton Abbey on Lady Day 1919 at the age of seven, where he has lived in the same house for the past 77 years. He was the sixth son and seventh child of a happy family with its roots in the country. In their smithy and garage, with the wide range of services and goods they provided, he was 'Jack of all trades'. Mainly he was considered to be 'the dressed up one' or "Thee wi' t'pen in t'back o' thee lug!". He drove their wagonnettes and taxis, helped with the fire-work in The Smithy, helped with the work on their small farm and organised their firms accounts. There have been few local committees down the years he has not served on, which meant he has always been at the centre of the planning and action in the area—a good place to be for an observant man with a dry sense of humour, an acute eye for detail and an astonishing memory.

He is Church Warden Emeritus at Bolton Priory, sang in the choir for 70 years and even 'officiated' at the Services held at the local Almshouses, deputising for the Priory Rector. He is an excellent fisherman, whose services to angling have been commemorated in a seat near Bolton Bridge. He also is a much appreciated raconteur!

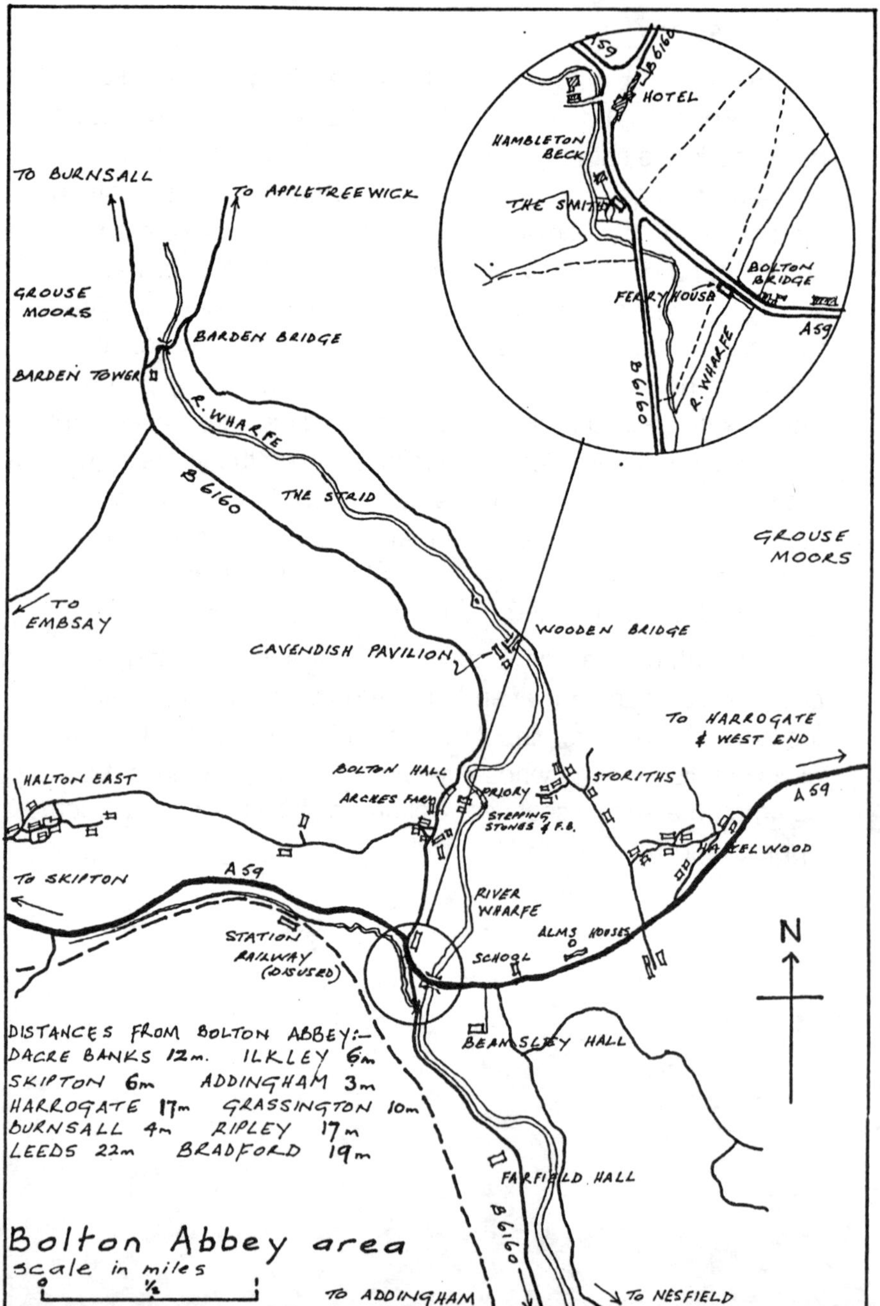

A59
B6160
HOTEL
HAMBLETON BECK
THE SMITHY
BOLTON BRIDGE
FERRY HOUSE
A59
B6160
R. WHARFE
TO BURNSALL
TO APPLETREEWICK
GROUSE MOORS
BARDEN BRIDGE
BARDEN TOWER
R. WHARFE
B6160
THE STRID
GROUSE MOORS
TO EMBSAY
WOODEN BRIDGE
CAVENDISH PAVILION
TO HARROGATE & WEST END
BOLTON HALL
HALTON EAST
STORITHS
A59
ARCHES FARM
PRIORY
STEPPING STONES & F.B.
HAZELWOOD
TO SKIPTON
A59
RIVER WHARFE
STATION
RAILWAY (DISUSED)
ALMS HOUSES
SCHOOL
N
DISTANCES FROM BOLTON ABBEY:—
DACRE BANKS 12m. ILKLEY 6m
SKIPTON 6m ADDINGHAM 3m
HARROGATE 17m GRASSINGTON 10m
BURNSALL 4m RIPLEY 17m
LEEDS 22m BRADFORD 19m
BEAMSLEY HALL
FARFIELD HALL
B6160
Bolton Abbey area
scale in miles
0
½
1
TO ADDINGHAM
TO NESFIELD

Contents

Acknowledgements

My grateful thanks are due to Val Rowell, for inspiration, encouragement, editing, chivvying, typing until all hours and for keeping the coffee pot on the boil.

With special thanks to His Grace, The Duke of Devonshire, for writing a foreword to the book and to Her Grace, The Duchess of Devonshire, the Marquess of Hartington and the Marchioness of Hartington who have given encouragement.

My thanks are also due to the many other people who have helped me in the preparation of this book and especially to: Philip Allon, Richard Bull, Paul Chipchase, Kelly Harte, Hannah Hauxwell, Godfrey Hicks, Derek Law, Kate Rhodes and Peter Watkins. Finally thanks to Carol Lambert for her care in the printing of the book.

Introduction

The location for this book is the village of Bolton Abbey in North Yorkshire which lies in the valley of the River Wharfe at National Grid Reference SD073539, 6 miles from the market town of Skipton, 5 from Ilkley, 17 from Bradford, 22 from Leeds and 16 miles from Harrogate. The village and the surrounding area have been the focal point from the 19th Century for many thousands of tourists, while landscape artists such as Turner, Cox, Girtin, Vicat-Cole and Herbert Royle have recorded some of its beauty on canvas.

The River Wharfe at Bolton Abbey winds between low, tree-lined hills and riverside pastures. Dry-stone walls built mainly from river cobbles, divide the fields and contain the grazing sheep and cattle. Heather topped moors with their grouse, pheasants and deer overlook the village and from these moor tops range upon range of hills can be seen.

The book however is about people who lived in Bolton Abbey in the hard but fascinating time between the two World Wars as viewed by the author and describes a community at peace. Mostly they were tenants, employees or pensioners on the Duke of Devonshire's large Bolton Abbey Estate but he has also written about the royal, rich or famous people who visited Bolton Abbey at that time. He brings the period to life with humorous or poignant anecdotes. His family's firm was based at the Smithy at Bolton Abbey from 1919 to 1971, which was then the hub of village life; so he was in a good position to write about local people and events.

The period between the wars was a time of change in the way people travelled, worked and played, since it was during this time that motor vehicles slowly replaced the horse, petrol-driven milking machines gradually became available, more cinemas were opened and the wireless began to provide home entertainment. The author has recorded some of the hardships endured, the pleasurable times and the effect of change.

Apart from the increase in traffic, a modern tourist would notice little change from the Twenties and Thirties. From the 'Hole in the

Wall', a gap in the massive boundary wall of Bolton Priory, they could overlook the partly ruined 12th Century Augustinian Priory with nearby Bolton Hall nestling within a sweep of the river. They might call at Forge Cafe or the garage next door about ¾ of a mile from the village green on the B6160 and wonder how it used to be. This was the site of the Smithy and the author's family business while their picturesque 16th Century cottage, 'Ferryhouse', lies next to the old A59 bridge over the Wharfe. It is still delightfully peaceful in Bolton Abbey. The only difference is that between the Twenties and Thirties tens of thousands of people used to visit, walking down Bolton Lane from the Station to the Priory and other beauty spots or travelled from the station by waggonette: now, arguably, fewer of them come but they come by car which is noisier. But even on the busiest day, off road, the scene is one of refreshment and tranquillity. The author hopes that the reader will sit back and enjoy this atmosphere of tranquillity, sense the hardship people experienced but also learn something about their life-style and humour.

Preface

I have been persuaded by Paul Chipchase (a Cambridge academic) and others to write about the halcyon times between the wars at Bolton Abbey since life has changed so dramatically for us all since that time. It was considered worth recording the struggle for some to live off the land, the humour, the contrasts in living standards and the way we coped with the rapid changes in technology. As far as possible I have presented the events in chronological order and I think you will find the presentation logical and,hopefully, humorous and interesting.

Since I was not born at Bolton Abbey but went to live there at Ferryhouse on Lady Day 1919, I will start by giving you some of my background before then.

I was born in 1912 at Dacre Banks in the valley of the River Nidd in North Yorkshire and was the sixth son and seventh child of Robert and Sarah Wood. My Father's family were farmers and millers in Nidderdale. He was a forester (what else with a name like Wood?) and served his apprenticeship with my maternal Grandfather, who was Head Forester in Birstwith, Nidderdale, and through whom he met my Mother.

Later he became Head Forester at Ripley Castle and my parents and five of us children lived in a lovely house which is now a saddlery shop. The most vivid memories of Ripley are starting school in a beautiful building opposite the 'Hotel de Ville'. I remember learning to ride a bicycle, making forbidden visits to the slaughterhouse and getting a tin fast on my head and a pea up my nose. But most fascinating were the visits to the village cobbler who kept a monkey who was trained to hammer the pre-soaked leather soft. The village children never tired of watching this operation. At Ripley my brother George learned his trade with the village blacksmith, my brother Harry joined the army and my sister worked in Harrogate in a furniture factory and later on munitions.

George started working for a Harrogate blacksmith, making iron corkscrew posts for barbed-wire entanglements for the army, so we moved to Harrogate. My Father got a job with the War Office in charge of Prisoners of War felling timber on the Castle Howard Estate, near Malton, East Yorkshire. We then took a cottage in Welburn and travelled to and from Harrogate, roughly 45 miles away, on a Rex-Acme motor cycle which was belt driven and had a basket work side-car.

The cottage we lived in was owned by the next door farmer and was situated between his village shop and the Crown and Cushion. Life in Welburn was interesting and varied. The proximity of a hundred acre field full of wicked, foreign prisoners of war was quite daunting, especially after dark as they were only contained by barbed wire.

Attending the village school, I fell violently in love with the infant teacher. She always wore a pale lilac overall, which is still my favourite colour. The last memories of that part of my life are ringing the school bell, which was almost too much for me to lift, to celebrate Armistice and listening to that vast army of prisoners encamped at Welburn singing all night to celebrate their forthcoming release from captivity.

Returning to Harrogate at the end of the Great War and living there meant attending school. I went to Christ's Church, a horrid 'towny' school with horrid 'towny' children. All I can remember of that period is being in constant floods of tears in a corner of the playground. As a result of my misery I was transferred to St Peter's School in the middle of town. Incredibly this school was even worse. Living in Harrogate had some compensations. It was possible to read by the gas lights with mantles. The Public Baths were nearby and George played in the Municipal Orchestra, which meant free admission to rehearsals.

The house we lived in was in a 'good' part of Harrogate, in a respectable street of large, stone-fronted houses, each with a small front garden surrounded by stone walls, topped with spiked railings. It had once been lived in by a Mayor of Harrogate! My sister got married when her fiance came home on leave from France and they moved to their own house. This was the signal for Father to start looking for somewhere more congenial for him since my Mother and their growing family were all country folk and not suited to suburbia—but where?

Chapter 1

Happy is the Man...

Psalm 127 Verse 5

Holding on tightly to my Father's Egyptian cloth motor-cycle jacket with the noise from the Rex Acme Vee Twin engine in my ears, I caught my first glimpse of Bolton Abbey as we came over the last rise from Harrogate on Lady Day 1919.

The sheer excitement of the day! We had actually left Harrogate, which I'd hated with every fibre of my being, and as a family set off to start a new life at Bolton Abbey. My two brothers Harry and George, Uncle Edwin and the furniture had gone before and with Mother in the wicker 'side-car' with my brother Jack, aged ten, and me, aged seven, riding pillion, Father had set off!

I was entranced by the 16th Century Ferryhouse in its situation by Bolton Bridge on the banks of the River Wharfe. It was quite roomy with four bedrooms for seven of us, my parents, Uncle Edwin, (Mother's invalid brother) three of my brothers and me.

I ran round the six acres of land rented from the Duke of Devonshire's Bolton Abbey Estate and explored every inch on that sunny Spring day with my brother Jack. George, a trained blacksmith, was to work in the Smithy so that was explored too. It was a very exciting place for small boys and one which as 'Woods' business developed would become the epicentre of village life, as someone recently put it.

On that first day we explored the road leading to Bolton Abbey village which had a few old cottages overlooking a village green. On the way we found a mysterious hollow tree which turned out to be a marvellous base for games and larks. On that first night I remember sleeping on a mattress with my parents in the sitting room. It was the first day of a new era for 'Woods'.

We had been living in Harrogate with my Father unemployed after his wartime job. He saw his future in Wharfedale or perhaps suitable jobs in that area had appealed to him and he had successfully applied for the tenancy of Ferryhouse, complete with smallholding, blacksmith's shop, orchard and farm buildings, which was everything he wanted.

Ferryhouse was just right for the family. My sister had married and settled in Harrogate. My eldest brother, Herbert, lived in Tyneside and another of my brothers had died while we lived in Dacre Banks. We all somehow fitted into the house and there was even a small, dark bedroom left over for visitors. The four sons occupied one bedroom with two double beds with little room for anything else. Jack and I were younger than George and Harry and we slept younger to older to each bed and listened to their grown-up conversations.

Ferryhouse had stone-flagged floors and a big stone sink with a cold-water tap. It had no running hot water or bathroom. The lavatory was outside and, unusually for the times, was a flushing type. Washing and shaving was done in a tin bowl on the sink. The women folk washed upstairs, using an earthenware bowl with a water-carrying jug to match on a marble-topped piece of furniture made for the purpose. The sole supply of warm water was from a side boiler, part of the kitchen range. On special occasions, such as the weekly bath-time, the water was heated in the built-in set pan (clothes boiler) which had a small coal fire underneath. Bathing was done in a life-sized galvanised bath kept in the shed for the purpose and was put on the home-made hearth rug in front of the kitchen fire—quite luxurious when the fire was good.

My Mother did everything in the house apart from a little help from one of the multitude of female cousins during the Summer and later from my sister in law, Rosamund. Mother cooked, made jam and marmalade, cleaned, decorated, mended, washed and ironed the clothes, made beds, cleaned shoes, made clothes, fed the hens, chopped kindling for the fires, did the gardening and even occasionally found time to go to Church. Jack and I were free to play bows and arrows or anything else we wished.

Mother, not content to simply look after her big family, built up a thriving Teas and Refreshments business, as did many more householders in the Parish. My Father built a pergola bower on the riverside lawn, festooned with rambler roses with a canvas top for wet days. Plain Teas (bread and butter, jam, scones, tea-cake, fruit cake etc.) for 1/3d were popular, as were 'Fruit Teas' ('Plain Teas' plus tinned fruit) at 1/6d. Pride of place was reserved for Ham Teas for 2/6d. Here they had a choice of boiled ham and salad and home-made cakes. Mother also ran a small sweet and cigarette shop, as other local people did. Many times customers would call on an evening, spend probably sixpence on cigarettes and sweets, stay for the evening, play dominoes or cards and stay for supper. Not particularly profitable but enjoyable.

George, the main blacksmith, was extremely skilled at fire work, and was also a skilled musician on brass, violin, piano, sang bass and became deputy organist at the Priory. He could consume prodigious quantities of bitter beer, tell tall stories and smoke or chew tobacco—sometimes simultaneously.

Harry became a forester on the Bolton Abbey estate; a job he kept for the rest of his working life. He was a singer, in big demand for oratorios and won competitive music festivals. He also became captain of the local cricket team. His forte was angling, dressing his own artificial flies, and his name is still a legend in Wharfedale for his upstream worming for grayling and as a teacher of angling.

In the early days, Jack and I were at school but later we joined the family firm based at our nearby Smithy, as blacksmith welder and bookkeeper respectively. Jack later became nationally and locally famous for his splendid branding irons, made for many purposes but mainly for branding the owner's initials onto the horns of moorland sheep. He also made many fine wind-vanes and had a good baritone voice, with many years in the Priory choir.

As time went on my Father's cup overflowed, with the firm doing well, my Mother's business thriving, all the rest of his family, as it happened, to remain so and the land for him to raise his pedigree Aylesbury ducks and Buff Rock hens. Not for him the selling of eggs for eating at a shilling a dozen but rather pedigree, fertile eggs for hatching at five times the price. He hatched some of the eggs in a battery of hatching boxes and two incubators and sold day-old chicks or ducklings. I was very proud when he bought pedigree cockerels from King George the Fifth's pedigree farm at Sandringham. Father advertised his poultry and had special boxes for dispatch of eggs or chicks by post or train.

We had two cows which provided milk, cream, butter and cheese for all the family, with enough to spare for near neighbours. Pigs provided bacon and ham for all the year and brawn, spare ribs and other delicacies at pig-killing time. The land also supported a horse to pull the farm cart and waggonette. My Father plied for hire with the latter from Bolton Abbey Station to the Priory and to the ornamental woods where a large cafe catered for the many visitors.

One Autumn Father bought 12 'shot' lambs at Barden Sheep Sale for 3/3d each. These were poor little lambs which had not thrived for some reason, such as losing the mother whilst still too young to wean or being fast in a thorn hedge for too long, or such. Father nursed these lambs all Winter and they improved considerably, unlike the market, which had worsened so much that the following Spring they were worth less than he had given for them!

It was not in Father's nature to take a loss without a struggle so he asked my brother-in-law in Harrogate to tout for orders for Spring lamb. John Cockshott of Beamsley killed and dressed them in return for the pelts. My brother-in-law duplicated on a jelly duplicator sheets like huge sheets of stamps. The tickets were required by law for butchers to affix to all joints of meat, stating, 'Bought of R. Wood . . . lbs . . . ozs. These were perforated for tearing off by my sister using her sewing machine without thread in it.

To replace the purpose-made miniature bayonet devices with which the ticket was attached to the meat by butchers, we straightened out and re-formed paper clips. All that remained was to tour Harrogate in the Ford Model T looking for customers' houses and braving the looks of any regular butchers who saw us.

Thus we all pursued our new ways and went about our work or play, except Uncle Edwin who was not strong enough for work. He had a fearful craving for rum and I went regularly to the Devonshire Arms for reinforcements of Monoplane Dark Rum which I think was 12/6d a bottle. I had strict instructions not to tell Mother but I am sure she knew. He passed some of his time riding round the district delivering 'pop' (mineral waters) on horse-drawn wagons with 'Professor' Pop Harrison of Addingham, who was a striking, gaunt man with an absent-minded air. He wore a stiff, starched, wing collar, known generally as a 'Come to Jesus' collar, and had the largest but one blackhead I have ever seen in his nose and wore a pair of pince nez spectacles on a black silk cord. He also ran the village chemist's shop so possibly his academic achievements lay in that direction.

In the early days Father always had one of us, either a man or a lad, available to take on any task which could earn an honest shilling and would get me out of bed by saying, "There may be a man coming on horseback who will want his horse holding and he might give you a shilling!". Each time Father called me he said it. I always believed him and got up right away because I wanted the money, but the man with the horse sadly never turned up! The jobs undertaken by one or other of the family included relief postman, verger, grave-digger, organist, chimney sweep, spare driver or driving instructor and assisting in the building of a Dutch Barn, since the farmer was afraid of heights. We didn't like them much either but we would ignore this difficulty to get paid for doing the job.

The Bible says of children, "Happy is the man who hath his quiver full of them, he shall not be ashamed when he stands with his enemy in the gate." I would paraphrase this, "Happy is the man who hath a man or a lad available when there is an opportunity to earn a shilling or two!" With the establishment of the Wood family at Ferryhouse and of the business at the Smithy with its community links, it created the opportunity for Jack and me to have an idyllic boyhood in the area.

Chapter 2

I know a bank whereon the wild thyme blows

William Shakespeare: 'A Midsummer Night's Dream' Act 2 Scene 2

Moving into Ferryhouse, an ancient Daleshouse full of interest, was like starting a new life. The River Wharfe lapped up the garden wall in Summer and sometimes in Winter came into the house, which was very exciting for a small boy but not for my parents who had to clean up and dry out. The river was fascinating from low water to the raging floods in Winter and all stages in between. It was a constant source of interest to the family when it was likely to flood the house. The colour varied between gin-clear and dark brown and the reflections were also constantly changing.

I soon became familiar with the fish population, trout and grayling, and aware of their feeding patterns and was fascinated by a 'good rise': another talking point with enthusiasts. I spent hours looking over the garden wall at feeding fish and lobbing bread, kneaded into a ball of the correct density or moistness to correct for the wind so that it hit the water about two feet above the fish's snout. The top fish, before they became invisible due to the shadow from Bolton Bridge, was always a good one. I soon discovered that a feeding fish occupies the same spot within very small limits of movement and another smaller fish feeds in the same slip-stream a few yards down-stream and moves up if the first fish is caught or moves away.

The six acres which my Father farmed and which became my private paradise was bounded on one side by the river and the other sides of the triangular shape of the property were bounded by roads with dry-stone walls. The land was divided into a small meadow and a pasture by a dry-stone wall and a thorn hedge and these fields were bisected by Hambleton Beck. This stream, about eight feet wide at Summer level and 12 inches deep, provided everything a boy could want. Where the dividing wall met the stream there was a water heck (flood gate) hanging on a stout pole and with feet on the swinging gate it was a perilous and exciting crossing place.

There was everything there, marsh marigolds in Spring, beds of water cress and in Summer the banks were covered with donkey-rhubarb so high that one could walk through it in the semi-gloom made by the large leaves and flush out all kinds of quarry, rabbits, water rats, waterhens, etc. The only animal that refused to scurry away on my approach was an otter with a litter of young. This stared at me, hissed and snarled and barked. I was very ready to detour.

Hambleton Beck had a good head of trout as fingerlings were put into the higher reaches by the beck watcher (water bailiff) every Spring. There were also countless shoals of minnows which, when disturbed, all moved in the same way as if they were joined by an invisible thread. Probing by hand amongst the stones on the bed, it was possible to catch bullheads and freshwater crayfish: the latter a delicacy of which we were not aware. Lying on the bank on a Summer day it was possible to catch trout by the method known as 'tickling' or they could be pinned to the bottom by a well-made thumb-stick. Such activities were frowned on by those in authority and some adults looked on it as 'not quite the thing to do!' There were however certain boys who carried on in spite of feelings of guilt!

The bird population on the river was just as interesting, the commonest being the waterhen. It was almost impossible to look down the stretch of river, seen from the kitchen window, without seeing one of these immaculate birds paddling serenely across. On one occasion I was horrified to see a waterhen seized from under the water by a predator. The hapless creature screeched, flapped frenziedly and tried to take off, but was held by one foot and eventually the uneven struggle ended and the poor bird disappeared under the water with only a few bubbles to mark its watery grave. It was only time I saw this happen and have wondered ever since what the predator could have been. Possibly a large pike would have been capable of doing this but there are no records of any coarse fish getting further up-stream than the mill dam at Addingham, two miles away.

Mallard were numerous and, dependent on the weather, usually had a long period of hatching and all Spring and Summer clutches of different sizes could be seen. The most fascinating were the 'day olds', even in the high water and in the rough water, sailing like a small flotilla being chivied by their mother, then when they were frightened they would run on the surface at incredible speed.

There were occasional visits from pairs of geese and more rarely swans. The latter never nested in this area but geese often nested below the house in a well hidden area of undergrowth well above the average flood level. Our larder was usually swelled by about four eggs from each nest found. To have taken more would have raised suspicion and probably made the birds desert the nest.

The bird would lay 12-14 perfect eggs over the period of a fortnight and then stop. During this time they left the nest every day to make sure that the goslings did not start to incubate before the bird had finished laying. Then they would sit for four weeks during the incubation period. If the bird sat on the nest throughout the laying and the four week incubation period then one gosling would hatch each day and the bird would have to sit on the nest for six weeks instead of four.

Always to be seen on my patch were two pairs of dippers, who invariably occupied the same territory and took it in turns to occupy a favourite stone, hunt for food or feed their young. Occasional visitors were goosanders, grebes and dab-chicks. The first time I saw a dab-chick disappear under the water I thought it had been taken by a more stealthy predator than the one that took the waterhen. I was much relieved when I saw it come to the surface and found out much later that these intrepid birds walked on the river bed in search of food. Pride of place was taken by the heron, that large mysterious and magnificent bird. It was often seen in the river shallows and in Hambleton Beck, mainly in the half-light of dawn or dusk.

One Summer two mallards made a double nest close to the river over the garden wall and always sat nose to tail. The river would only have to have risen a matter of inches to have flooded their nest. However they were good weather forecasters or their instincts were correct as they were perfectly safe for the whole of the four weeks. Another mallard built its nest in a perpetual candytuft plant on the top of the high riverside wall which was level with the lawn. It was a very brave bird and took no notice when we went near to the nest or went past it with the lawn mower. There was an extremely high flood at hatching time which got to within a few inches of its nest. The ducklings started to hatch at the height of the flood and I was anxious to see what they would do as they usually take to the water immediately.

On the Saturday night it appeared that they had almost all hatched but on the Sunday afternoon I looked round for them and was amazed to find them on Hambleton Beck. I could not imagine how they had got there as I thought it impossible that they had swum down the river, then up Hambleton Beck in the flood. Nor could I believe that they had walked across the fields, as very young ducklings 'drown' in wet grass. By whatever means, there they were in the calm where two streams met. They had found a submerged, waterlogged, compartmented mineral water crate which was laid on its side and they were investigating the bottle compartments.

On another occasion a waterhen made a nest on a log-jam nearby and was in no danger from a rising river until hatching time. The river started to rise and as usual bits of straw and driftwood and such material came down, which started to catch on the logs below the nest and the cock bird kept towing them out into the stream as they looked as if they might become a hazard. These tactics were reversed when the flood got higher: the cock started collecting these bits of flotsam and with the help of its mate built up the nest several inches, taking up the eggs one at a time. Unfortunately they were overtaken and the whole structure washed away.

Other than the otter confronted under the donkey rhubarb, I only saw four more, one of them being dead on the bank. One came out of the river opposite Ferryhouse and walked up the bank before it disappeared up a land drain and though I watched the area for hours it never reappeared. The others only appeared as a wake on the river surface at the point of which a small nose appeared. One evening on the point of dark I was fishing with one of my brothers and, seeing an otter wake approaching, I moved my elbow very cautiously to draw his attention, but it was still sufficient to turn the wake in the other direction.

Rabbits were plentiful and on many farms, especially with river banks where the ground was sandy and good to burrow they were a scourge, eating or foiling most of the growth. Many methods of catching them were employed but their numbers were never significantly reduced. They were bolted by ferrets and shot or caught in nets and the Estate Beck Watcher's job during the trout close season was mainly rabbiting.In those hard days rabbits were a cheap source of meat and most working class families had rabbit pie and stew quite regularly, which was a tasty, hearty meal when well done. The Estate workers of the period were paid fortnightly and each received a brace of rabbits with their wages in Winter.The legendary figure, Richard Fawcett, 'Rabitty Dick', who got more than his share, was a local railway worker who spent all his spare time poaching and the stories of his escapes from the keepers were hair-raising and legendary. Later in life he made his name by writing his memoirs in a series of books. I only once saw a rabbit enter the river on the opposite bank to Ferryhouse and swim to the opposite bank in a fairly big river. I ran down the bank to see it emerge and to prove it was in fact a rabbit. It was not pursued and I never came to any conclusion for this unusual behaviour.

Apart from the edible water cress growing in the unpolluted water of Hambleton Beck, plant life, edible and decorative, abounded for most of the year: marsh marigolds on the waterside, drifts of primroses on the banks, ragged robins under the hedges, cowslips in the meadow and not far away, masses of bluebells.

Edible plants were more interesting to me and my friends. We ate the first fresh shoots of hawthorn and for some reason it was always called 'bread and cheese'. Beech mast was gathered in great numbers to glean the minute, edible centre. Blackberries, usually called brambles or 'bumblekites' were a prize crop. They always grew in woodland after the mature trees had been felled and for some years before the newly planted trees robbed them of light: marvellous to think they had lain dormant for years. Acorns were eaten sparingly since too many didn't agree! Small smokable pipes were made with the husk with straw for the stem, hay-seeds being used for tobacco, which my friend Fred Rennard and I smoked under the small bridge over Hambleton Beck on Ferryhouse land. Fred and I also occasionally smoked Woodbines, five for 2d! The greatest disgrace was to be sick in front of our friends. Afterwards we ate grass, which we thought took away the smell. Spreading out my catchment area beyond my miniature paradise, miniature strawberries abounded on the railway banking, enough to take home for tea given enough patience.Prize raspberries were also there in abundance and the seeds were said to have been carried there by birds feeding in the garden of the nearby Farfield Hall. The bankings of the railway line were deliberately burned every Spring to keep the growth low so as to avoid a big fire if the bankings were ignited by a spark from a train and this practice ensured these food crops thrived year after year.

In the nearby Lob Wood was a wet and boggy area with a clay pit which teemed with tadpoles and frogs in season and provided clay, collected annually for sealing the house flood boards. My Father also used clay for the cows to kneel on as they lay down or stood up when fastened in the mistal for Winter, as he said it was kinder to their knees and avoided 'big knee', a common ailment in cows.

The Beck was a constant source of delight. My friends and I built quite elaborate dams and when there were sufficient of us we 'drove' the fish upstream and enjoyed watching them wriggle up the dam like a migration of salmon. The first flood always washed the dam away but we had all the time in the world to build another and better one.We had quite impractical ideas of generating electricity which never got beyond the planning stage. We were goaded on in this pursuit as the mains electricity was not yet available and we knew that there were supplies made by turbines, although most of the big houses were supplied by a dynamo and paraffin engine.

All the farming on Ferryhouse land was done by hand apart from mowing the hay and I enjoyed virtually every job. The only jobs I did not like were muzzling the ferret and extracting the teeth of the piglets.

The liquid effluent from the mistal when the cows were tied up for Winter, or when they were being milked, flowed through the wall behind them, through a pipe into a catchment dish which also carried roof water from a down pipe. This waste of such precious fluid was too much for my Father who re-directed the roof water and sank a barrel to catch the effluent. This was emptied with a bucket attached to a pole and carried into another barrel suspended on a Smithy-made conveyance made specially for the purpose with pulling handle and iron wheels. Dispensing this with a bucket was a smelly job but very effective, the blue/green new growth showing through very quickly, especially in a 'growy' time. I hit upon a bright idea after seeing in a book the enormous 'White Horse of Kilburn'. In a more modest way I marked upon a prominent hillside in the meadow, my initials in effluent intertwined with those of my girl-friend Rosie Hamilton. This was a great success and being readily visible from the main road was the subject of much comment. How romantic being linked in liquid manure!

Chapter 3

Il faut noter, que les jeux d'enfants ne sont pas jeux et les faut juger en eux comme leurs plus serieuses actions

(It should be noted that children at play are not playing about; their games should be seen as their most serious-minded activity)

'Essais' (1580) ed. M.Rat, (1958) bk.1, Ch. 28 of his friend Etienne de la Boetie.

Michel Eyquem de Montaigne.

In my Pre-teen years I was dressed, as were all my contemporaries, in an almost uniform manner, in 'long' shorts of some rough material. On top we wore a woolly jumper usually referred to as a 'gansy', no doubt a corruption of 'Guernsey'. These jumpers were almost always a dull grey, often made of re-constituted wool from other garments which had been unravelled. They always had sleeves and turn-down collars with a band of lighter colour. Knee length stockings had turn-down tops, again with a lighter coloured band on them. These were held up by elastic which, when new, made a corrugated pattern on our legs, so quite often stockings were pushed down for comfort.

Footwear was always boots. No-one wore shoes, but sometimes the 'pumps' we had to have for P.T. at school were worn. I would have given anything for a pair of 'hill-farmer's boots', hand-made by George Whittaker's of Addingham. These waterproof boots had curled-up toes for walking up steep fields. They had lace- holes to within an inch of the toes and strong leather laces. To make these boots totally waterproof they had what we called 'bellases', (bellows?) as the tongues which were attached in such a way to keep out the water looked rather like a pair of bellows.

Long trousers were never worn until boys left school at 14 and my first pair were a complete disaster. I nattered my mother for a pair long before she thought I should wear them. She ordered a pair from a travelling packman draper who was a cunning man. He realised from what my Mother said that I desperately wanted to 'grow-up' and, opportunist that he was, he sent a suit in the most hideous cloth and colour, knowing that in my urgency I would overlook these shortcomings. My first outing in it was to Evensong at the Priory. Fortunately it was dark, and wearing my longest coat pushed as far down as I could, by stooping forward, I crept into the back pew. My mates soon found out my secret and ragged me without mercy and were quick to point out the horrors of my new suit.

Wellingtons hadn't been invented when I was a youngster. What I would have given to be able to play in Hambleton Beck without coming home with wet socks and boots and getting into trouble each time while Mother put them by the fire to dry out. But the days were full of interest and fun for children of my age growing up in the twenties.

We amused ourselves with bird-nesting, cycling, shooting with air-guns or catching minnows or small trout but we were often pretty well fully employed helping on the farm or in the garden. We played 'cowboys', marbles occasionally, bowling and hoops, at which I excelled, with a special tool made by my blacksmith brother, George, which could be used for bowling or braking. The boys had bows and arrows and spent much time looking in the nearby woods for suitable wood to make them. Rounders were played in mixed teams, both in P.T. and in free time.

Most time was spent making houses against the wall of the wood we used to play in. The 'throughs' of the wall (large stones which were wider than the wall and placed at intervals to stabilise it) were used to display little 'ornaments', pictures were put on the walls and in our imagination they were desirable dwellings. Sliding on concrete in hobnailed boots with the accompanying sparks was almost equal to snow and ice slides in the Winter. Whips and tops had a brief season but did not last. The only outings we made were to the woods, the Priory and the school.

One profitable pastime especially in Summer, was gleaning under the railway station platform at Bolton Abbey for coins dropped accidentally which had slipped between the wooden boards. So many passengers passed through the station that a very small percentage of 'butterfingers' made for rich pickings. We approached the platform when all was quiet at the farthest end from the offices and entered through the complex under the platform and grubbed about, keeping very quiet and feeling liable to being spotted through the gaps in the boards. On a good day we could get a few shillings, but it was a red-letter day when we found a half-crown, which was more than a month's pocket money.

Many boys were in the Priory choir and had to attend practices on Wednesday nights and there were Sunday-School trips and choir trips, choir concerts and choir suppers as well as morning and evening services on a Sunday. Billiards and card games were played in the Cavendish Institute in Bolton Abbey village. The Institute had a purpose-built billiard room and a library, with an outside gasworks to provide light. The billiard table was full size and a long, raised upholstered seat was provided for spectators. Those waiting for a game played card games, using matches for wagers. The reading room was largely unused although it had been popular in an earlier time when newspapers were not so common. It was used as a library one evening a week and for various meetings. The Institute was a gift of a former Duke of Devonshire. Later it was made into an Estate Office and enlarged and a new village hall was built.

The housekeeper from the Duke's Bolton Hall and the Agent's wife gave regular instruction to girls of the village who were members of the Girls' Club, a local organisation, in all branches of housework and handicrafts. Poker work was very popular and most houses in the area had examples of this craft. Plain, whitewood boxes of every sort were bought and decorated by scorching patterns with the poker which was a platinum tipped tool. It was heated by methylated spirits and fanned to produce more heat by a pipe attached to a rubber bellows held in the palm of the hand.

Each season brought its own interests. In Spring, dormant hedgerows and trees got new life: eagerly awaited field and garden flowers started to show and blossom on apple trees. Damson and blackthorn bore promise of fruits to come. Lambs appeared early in spite of the possibility of late, bad weather so as to be ready for an early market with top prices. (Government guaranteed prices not having been thought of). Trout started to appear in the beck and river and, in warm weather and sometimes in cold, fish began to rise to the fly. Birdnesting had to take second place to the jobs Father always found for me to do.

Manure was taken direct into our fields each day in a wheelbarrow and then emptied into heaps in straight rows and at even intervals so that a skilled operator, usually me, could stand at the heap and spread it with a gripe (fork) in such a manner that the whole field was covered reasonably evenly and without any bare patches.

Much more memorable was chain-harrowing the field, with harrows made in our own blacksmith's shop, using some worn-out non-skid chains from a motor-wagon and pulled by our ex-War Department horse, Dick. The leather reins which were part of Dick's harness were far too short for this operation as I walked behind the harrows, so they were replaced by ploughing 'strings'. These appealed to me enormously. I can only think that it was the thought of controlling a large animal with such a slender cord, or perhaps it was because horse-breakers used them. I looked with awe on men breaking-in horses as they were always young horses and often frisky and unpredictable.

Summer brought many delights, including hay-making which, although hard work, was pleasant if the weather was good, especially the 'drinking times'. Mother always brought the food and drink to us, even when we were working near to the house. This must have been part of her loving because when we were sitting in the sun under a wall or with our back to a sweet-smelling hay-cock devouring her home-made ham sandwiches, tea-cakes, jam pasties and apple pies with hot, sweet tea or nettle beer, she just smiled at us.

Activities in the beck really got going when we were able to paddle bare-foot in the deeper waters and chilly swimming, on even hot days, was possible in the river. My friends and I spent countless hours making rafts and it would have been like a Mediterranean cruise if we had ever managed one that would float, especially with one of us on board. Quite often we used empty oil-drums which always needed a hole repairing with solder. This was never a success but it is sad that when later in life I was able to solder I had no desire to make a raft.

One Summer when I was about ten most of my friends had bicycles and I started to 'badger' my Mother to get one for me. I had my eye on a Rudge Whitworth which I had seen in a cycle shop in Skipton. It had distinctive Rudge-style pointed mudguards and coupled brakes; a very doubtful benefit, I gathered from owners who had been catapulted over the handlebars. However, no Rudge for me. For some reason Mother went with my brother George to Otley, ten miles away and bought a lady's cycle for me for ten shillings! Imagine my horror; not only a lady's model but it had a dress guard to stop skirts getting in the back wheel. It also had a strange looking saddle labelled "Doctor Warnet's Patent Pneumatic Ladies' Saddle" —I can see it now; the name is etched in my memory! A final indignity was permanently fixed handlebar grips, while the 'fashion' among the other boys of my age was to have push-on, ex-army, gas-mask corrugated tubing. My friends found plenty to say about my new bike! I was a long time forgiving my Mother, but eventually I enjoyed the freedom and forays into new territory.

In a good season, Autumn brought its crop of fruits on trees and bushes, either to be picked from one's own land or stolen from some neighbour's land or garden, the latter always tasting better. Father surveyed the area when he first came to Bolton Abbey and found it largely fruitless. To rectify this he went to sales of trees in Harrogate each Winter and not only set a good example by planting fruit trees on his own land but encouraged and bullied his neighbours to do likewise and many locals today enjoy the result of his energies. He not only sold plants and trees, varieties of apple, plums (mainly damson greengage and Victoria) but also raspberries, gooseberries and rose-trees and was prepared to see that they were correctly planted. As a result, quite often his customers would ask him to come and see and admire the crops and I went with him. I had tastings as well, sometimes followed by stomach ache! Firewood was gathered in readiness for hard weather to come and was sawn with a cross-cut saw, six or eight feet long and worked by two men or lads. The trick was that each man pulled in turn, never pushed, as this only made the blade buckle and slowed the work down.

Toward the end of Autumn, as the days shortened, the paraffin lamps put away for Summer were brought out, cleaned and polished, paying special attention to the glass, wicks trimmed, filled up and made ready. The light from these lamps before the advent of mantle lamps and pressurised lamps was minimal but the first high tea by lamp-light was quite an occasion. When the kitchen range had a good toasting fire with glowing coke without smoke, Mother was often asked if we could have toast for tea. What toast! Home-made bread, crisp on the outside and soft inside with home-made butter and preserves. Occasionally kippers were cooked in the same way with oil dripping into the ashes in the hearth.

Winter brought its own delights. Frost was always welcome and many people went skating on the fish-rearing ponds or on the lake in the discontinued local quarry and occasionally on the river in extreme conditions, but this was hazardous since as the water went down, the ice sloped to the middle of the river and cracked ominously. Sledging was fun but sliding on the roads was best. Snow was not melted by the Highway Authorities since salt was not used and the surface became better and better for sliding as it was flattened by traffic and the grit which was put on for better grip soon bedded in. One particularly good slide was made on the old Bolton Bridge, near Ferryhouse and improved as I and three friends slid in our hobnail Winter boots. It was the 'fritter' season and Mother made these delicacies fried in deep fat, over a 'Roarer Primus Stove'. These were made of a thickish, sweet batter and filled with sultanas or other fruits and by careful organisation and timing we were able to report to the kitchen after two 'runs' at exactly the right time to be given a hot fritter straight from the pan, scrumptious.

The cows were brought inside and tied up for months, only being let out once a day to drink from the trough. On our own small farm we only had two milk cows and I often went at milking time with Father or one of my elder brothers. My job was to hold the tail of the cow being milked as they had the habit of slashing them to each side in turn and as they were always wet, or sticky or both, this was unpleasant for the operator. I never remember the bigger farmers being so overmanned that they had a tail-holder. Milking time at Haw

Pike where I spent a lot of time, had one mistal for about twenty cows but was warm and intimate, especially for the milkers who had their capped heads buried in the cow's warm flanks and their usually bare arms and hands under the warm bellies and udders. My friend, Fred Rennard from Haw Pike, when he was helping to milk used to direct the cow's milk straight into the mouth of the cat, who always sat nearby waiting for this to happen. The noise of the cows eating or chewing the cud, fidgeting and rattling the chains by which they were fastened, lowing or mooing when the wind was howling outside, was magic to my ears.

Deep and drifting snow was exciting. I remember one evening during supper-time, there was a lull in the conversation and Father remarked on the absolute quiet outside and opening the door, oh bliss, there was a yard of snow across the doorway. White frosts were very beautiful: even mundane things like old nettle stalks turned into fairy wands and cobwebs in the hedgerows took on a magic look. Our penalty to pay for all these delights was chapped hands and inner legs and chilblains. The only cure, and not very effective, was glycerine and many nights I had to wear chamois gloves to protect the bedclothes. No concessions were made to the weather by wearing extra clothing, other than a scarf which was long and tickly and went round the neck, under the arms and was tied at the back.

A very special Winter treat was when one was allowed to spend time in the dark with the night-watchman on road-works. The watchman's job was to trim the warning lights around the trenches or obstructions, to see that they did not blow out on wild nights and to keep an eye on the workmen's tools and equipment. He stayed in his sentry box all night. What joy we thought not to have to go to bed. He surrounded himself with food boxes, packets of cigarettes and had an ingenious, double-ended tin: removing the lid at one end revealed sugar and the other, dry tea. Regular brews of smoked tea were made with boiling water from a kettle on the glowing brazier and had a smoked, brackish taste. Frosty nights and snow made these trips all the more exciting. We poked the brazier to greater output and heaped on County Council coke as if it were free.

Sometimes in the early evening, the watchman paid us 2d to fetch him fish and chips from Addingham and on return these were warmed up and often burned on a shovel over the fire. For many years the last job of the day for the farm man at the Bolton Abbey Devonshire Arms was to yoke the horse into the milk float and collect the evening newspapers for the guests from Bolton Abbey Station. My friends and I used to join him on this trip, which seemed particularly exciting on Winter evenings with the carriage lamps lighted.

The bedrooms were terribly cold and often in the very cold weather my breath condensed on the blankets and made blobs of ice which melted very uncomfortably when snuggling down. Horses took over again from the early motor vehicles and the roads were cleared by vee-shaped wooden snow-ploughs pulled by two horses.

The ploughs were parked when not in use at strategic points and the local farmers were authorised to use them when necessary. Thus my small 'Paradise' provided interest in every season and weather and all around were woods and hills and moors, all with their own bird, animal and plant life waiting for exploration as I grew into manhood.

Chapter 4

Strawberries swimming in the cream and schoolboys swimming in the stream

George Peele, 'Old Wive's Tale'; 1:75 (Song)

As a small boy in Bolton Abbey I attended the local Beamsley, Boyle and Petyt School. It was a small intimate school consisting of the main classroom with a smaller, infant room at right-angles at one end. There was a small entrance hall and cloakroom with a kitchen range. A front door on the West front opened onto a small vestibule above which was a belfry, but I cannot recall the bell ever being rung. This door was never used except by the girls to reach their toilet. The building was on a windy hillside and was geographically in the centre of the area it served; Bolton Abbey, Catgill, Hambleton, Beamsley, Storiths, Hazelwood and many outlying farms and homesteads. The school was endowed with money left by Robert Boyle, the scientist and enunciator of Boyle's law, as well as from moneys left by the two members of the Petyt family of Hazelwood, who made good as lawyers in London. When it was built in 1875 it replaced four former schools in the area.

The number of pupils whilst I was there varied between 50 and 55, who were accommodated in the two classrooms. The main body of the building was for seniors, aged between 7-14, with the children occupying different corners according to age. The 'top classroom' was for infants and was literally two steps higher than the adjacent senior room. The girls' cloakroom doubled as a kitchen and store-room. It contained rows of racks with hooks for hats and coats, with the kitchen range on one wall for drying clothes, etc., with a box used to store items at one end of the room. Monitors lingered in this cosy room. Food for those who lived too far away to go home for dinner, not 'lunch', consisted mainly of sandwiches, lots of pastry, onion, potato pasties, etc.

There was a School House for the use of the Headmistress, while the school caretaker at that time lived in a small cottage owned by the Estate. Nowadays the caretaker lives in the School House. The infant teacher was Miss Bertha Atkins, a Bolton Abbey woman, and Miss Agnes Townson from nearby Chelker Farm taught the seniors. They were both kindly and dedicated. Miss Townson took over from a relief teacher, Miss Jackson, and arrived with her dog, Jack, his kennel and her hand-luggage in a milk-float driven by her father. Miss Jackson had been a relief teacher for so long that she had really settled in, so much so that she had a flock of hens behind the school. She also kept a broody hen with 12 chicks in school in a coop and run. These were not for biology but to replace her flock. We had to move the chicken pen each day to a clean bit of floor and scrub the plot vacated. These chores and many others were always preferable to school-work and competition to log the daily temperature chart or water bits of carrot growing in saucers, attend to the tadpoles and such was fierce.

There was no school uniform. The girls were always swathed in an overall or 'pinny' while the boys invariably wore their woollen 'gansies', which were usually darned at the elbow, and their fairly long 'short' trousers. The village policeman's son, Percy Robertshaw, Winter and Summer, wore black woollen stockings, so long that they disappeared up the legs of his trousers which helped him to avoid the misery of chapped inner legs in cold weather. All the time I knew him he also wore an unusual hat, made of material which had a hole in it through which a tuft of hair sprouted. All the children walked to school. Many walked across fields or unmade roads and most had dirty or wet footwear. The children from Broadshaw, a lonely, distant farm, lodged during the week at the Pink Cottage, an old Toll-bar house demolished in 1941, next to the Smithy. Others stayed at times with relatives who lived nearer.

At the starting time the hand-bell was rung, for which there was great competition and we all gathered in neat rows on the concrete near the door. On the command, 'Quick march', a remnant of the recently ended Great War, we went into school. We took off our boots and put on woolly or felt slippers, made on the premises so as to keep the floor clean. Lessons then started, except for the lucky 'Fire Monitor' who spent as long as he or she dared attending to the fire of the cloakroom kitchen range on which a kettle was boiled for brewing up at dinner time and the oven for warming up food. One sought-after task was lighting the hanging paraffin lamps on a dark, Winter's day. The light they gave, being wick lamps, was minimal but they looked cosy and smelled . . .!

To invoke a spirit of healthy competition we were divided into 'houses' named after the Discoverers of the period. I was a Shackleton. Each House had distinctive, coloured arm-bands to wear when playing games. The Shackletons were yellow, an unhappy choice. On Friday afternoons we had an inter-house spelling competition, the winners being allowed out half an hour early and as it was necessary for families to leave together they all had to be in the same house. We Shackletons had the misfortune to include the Hibbert family in our ranks. They could not spell a word of two or three letters and were very unpopular on Fridays. In spite of this they did very well and the two boys emigrated to Australia to make their fortunes.

The boys formed into gangs and most of them took the matter very seriously. To my shame I was reported to the head of my gang, Mick Hamilton, for speaking to a member of a rival gang, which was absolutely forbidden. Mick walked down the road to intercept me as I walked to school and berated me at great length about loyalty, friendship and decency and even cried at one period, he was so overcome by my treachery.

I neither knew or cared what girls thought, said or did at that time and spent most of my spare time with my friend Fred Rennard, doing man's work. We made out countless lists of the guns, traps, stores and special clothing we would require when we became trappers in some Canadian waste.

To determine who was going to hide when playing 'hide and seek' or who was going to be 'It' for other games, whoever happened to be 'leader' used a jingle. They would point to the children standing in a row or a circle and repeat in a dull voice: *"Eleanor Mason broke a basin, How much will it be? Half a crown, Set it down, Out goes she/he!"*

Eleanor Mason from Broadshaw was on reflection just a bit older than me and an excessively pretty girl, not that we noticed at the time of course. I wonder was she pleased to have her name quoted like this? ('Set it down' in normal parlance meant make a note of it or put it on my bill).

Most boys and some girls sent off a postal order for one shilling to some entrepeneur in London who made us members of the 'True Blue Brotherhood'. He sent us a badge and various documents authenticating our membership and code-books for our exclusive use. If a friend was being mobbed by non-members we would shout the word, "Caterpillar!", which meant, we are going to attack your enemies from the rear! We had copies of two cycle catalogues. One was 'Moorhouses of Padiham', the other came from Burnley. These catalogues which had everything from complete bicycles to the smallest nut and bolt were pored over until they almost disintegrated. Sweets of all kinds were always referred to as 'spice'. We would say to anyone lucky enough to have a supply, "Gi' us a spice". Words were never ended, thus the 'v' and 'e' were omitted from 'give'. Singular and plural were often mixed, as 'us' for 'me' and 'they was' or 'he were'.

One day each Spring was Egg Collection Day, when everyone brought eggs to be given to Ilkley Coronation Cottage Hospital where they, like most local families, preserved them for use in Winter in a solution called 'water glass'. The eggs were placed in buckets or similar containers and the solution preserved them by sealing them to exclude air. The hens each family kept obeyed natural laws, like wild birds and were in full lay in Spring and stopped almost entirely in Winter, so the Spring glut helped out in the lean months.

The days before Christmas were always special, making paper chains and other decorations and discipline was relaxed. The big day of the year however was the Annual Prizegiving. Prizes were presented by the Duchess of Devonshire, Duchess Evelyn, who was usually accompanied by one or more of her daughters. We would rehearse for weeks walking from our places to a stand-in 'Duchess', a giggling, embarrassed schoolgirl. We bowed or curtsied and then said "Thank you, Your Grace". We then paused to reply to any remarks she might make, then returned to our seats. It was amazing how many ways there were to get it wrong on the day. I cannot recall anyone saying anything audible or of substance in reply to her remarks.

The Revd. C.F. Tomlinson came one morning a week to give us religious instruction and every Wednesday after school to rehearse the boys who were in the Priory choir. The latter was an occasion not to be missed as he distributed sweets from what he called 'a bag of lollipops' after every practice. Miss Townson could have us all sitting quiet as mice with our scalps tingling as she read to us. Unfortunately for her she had a stiff neck and could not turn her head quickly, so when she did not have our full attention, by the time she turned her head to see what we were up to, we had time to stop doing it. Her stiff neck seemed to date from her accident at the village dance held at the school. As the school was used for village dances the floor had to be made slippery by scattering French Chalk on it but Miss Townson slipped and broke her ankle. After that dance the floor had to be thoroughly scrubbed, much to the disappointment of the children.

All the children left school at fourteen, well prepared for life with all the basics of learning. One absolute essential implanted in many children who went to the school was an enquiring mind. Some girls who left school at 14 still came to school for a time to teach the smallest children for no pay. This amazed most 'big' boys who could not wait to leave, neither could they imagine anyone being so fond of small children, nor their desire to be a teacher. These non-stipendiaries were the children of better-off parents who were not pressing for them to be earning or to be doing 'men's work' on the home farm. A number of the pupils went on to the Grammar Schools at Ilkley or Skipton and I was one of them.

Chapter 5

And then the whining schoolboy, with his satchel and shining morning face, creeping like snail unwillingly to school

W. Shakespeare 'As You Like It' Act 2 Sc.2.

After many happy years at the Boyle and Petyt School at Beamsley I won a County Minor Scholarship in 1924 to Ermysted's Grammar School in Skipton and with some trepidation started there in September of that year. There were however some seven or eight boys that I knew who went to the school and some were deputed to look after the new boys, which helped. When I got my school 'togs' it was the first time I had any kind of head-gear which made me feel very self-conscious. The cap and tie were our main 'uniform' but those who could afford it could wear a blazer; the rest of us wore suits, either shorts or long trousers as we got older with a jacket and waistcoat.

At Bolton Abbey Station, on the way to school, Robert Demaine, Charles Beevers, Robert Wilson and I would gather waiting for the 08.20 Skipton train and in a separate group, Kathleen Whitaker, Kathleen Heseltine and Nelly Heseltine who were travelling to Skipton Girls' High School. Although there would only be one or two other people on this train there would be more on Mondays, market day in Skipton, and we all knew each other. If we got to the station early we had the excitement of seeing Bert Heseltine driving the milk float with a fast, sure-footed mare, rushing to catch the 08.10 to Ilkley, tearing round the corner into the station yard. On one occasion he did this so fast that he turned the float over, upsetting all the milk over the station approach. Sometimes there would be calves sewn into sacks waiting to be loaded into the guards van to be taken to the market.

The Station Master, Mr Dingle, always seemed imperious in his blue railway uniform and gold-braided hat with his waxed moustache, walking about seeing that things were in order. The porters, Winterburn and Jackson, would occasionally casually jump down from the platform, stroll across the line on the approach of a train and just as casually climb up the other side, something we would never have dared to do. We would look down the line at the sound of the whistle of the approaching train which would roar into the station with much steam, shrieking of brakes and rattling of carriages and then climb into our compartment, boys in one, girls in another. Once on the train, of course there were high-jinks. Little ones were sometimes lifted onto the netting luggage rack and we often took the sticks out of the roller blind to fence with. On one occasion Robert Wilson went out of the door of the carriage when the train was going through Haw Bank, Embsay, tunnel, walked along the running board and got into the girls' carriage.

The journey was by train all the four years I was there, with the exception of the General Strike, when we were forced to use the newfangled bus service. The Skipton bus was a Ford Model T with about 20 seats and usually had a hard top with glass side windows. It was fitted with an extra four-speed gear box in addition to the standard equipment of two band gears, making a total of eight gears. Even in the lowest gear it was short on power and on market days, with a full load, the fit had to disembark at the bottom of steep hills and walk and the very fit and the young had to push. It was a relief when the trains started again.

I was very proud of my quarterly pass for the train and longed to use it for other than school journeys but as we had a five and a half day school week there was little opportunity. The walk from the station to and from school was by the Leeds-Liverpool Canal bank, over the swing bridge and on Brook Street. Walking on the tow-path we were able to look down into a dentist's surgery and took delight in pulling 'agonised' faces at the patients. This room is still used by my dentist but in the intervening 60 years or so the view has been obscured by net curtains and the chair faces the opposite way. The English Sewing Company's mill backed onto the canal and regular loads of coal were delivered by horse-drawn barges.

One day, running to catch the train after doing detention, I was with Robert Wilson of Intake Farm, about four miles from Bolton

Abbey. Robert was very fit, as one would expect when he cycled daily from that remote farm to the station and back each evening. To my horror, the swing-bridge was turned to allow a coal barge through. The intrepid Robert, both fit and fearless, jumped onto the coal, ran across the barge and jumped to the other side. Unlike Robert I was fat rather than fit and frightened rather than fearless. I hesitated, jumped, landing onto the coal, but I sank into it. By the time I had plunged to the other side the barge was again in the full width water and too far for me to jump. The bargee deliberately steered a middle course, I think to teach me a lesson for my cheek. By the time he steered to the side at the unloading point my train had gone and I had no option but to walk the six and a half miles home.

On a happier note, 'Ma Pat' had a small tuck shop in the front of her house in Brook Street and when 'in funds' it was possible to buy such delicacies as Mint Imperials, Toasted Tea-cakes (small, round, chewy sweets covered with coconut) or Jap desserts. These were cubes of a coconut mixture, about 9/16ths x 9/16ths", covered with a pliable, sugary coating in a range of colours.

The school had been recently enlarged by the addition of several ex-army huts, each warmed by a single, central, round, cast-iron stove with a pattern on the lid. If it was possible to get a new boy to sit on the lid long enough or alternatively to put a boy on and restrain him long enough, a permanent pattern was embossed on the trouser seat. I managed to avoid having it done to me but later on I helped to do it of course.

At that period all the masters wore gowns and mortar boards and discipline was in the main strict and each master carried a cane to emphasise this. After the limited subjects taught at the Boyle and Petyt School, languages, physics and chemistry stretched our young minds and masses of homework for the first time hampered our evening and weekend activities. Most of the younger masters wore sports jackets under their gowns with leather patches on the elbows and soft leather binding on the cuffs. They often wore dark flannels and mostly, good, strong shoes. This garb must have made a lasting impression on boys of my period as most of us still dress this way. The headmaster, Mr McIntosh was stern but fair. He, like the other masters, wore his robes and mortar board and administered the cane for punishment he had decided to mete out and also on their behalf.

The masters varied tremendously in discipline from very strict to those who had given in totally. Many of them seemed old, past retiring age. Perhaps teachers were in demand due to fewer being available since so many young men were killed during the First World War. The rest of the masters were quite young and still full of enthusiasm. Dear, kindly Mr Clements who taught Geography and Divinity, long due for retirement, had a hard time of it with the undisciplined. For Art classes we attended the Science and Art School in Skipton High Street, which was an opportunity for larking about, but the teacher, Miss Fanny Shuttleworth, daughter of the Principal, had our complete attention. She was a quiet, gentle lady and we were all in love with her. I learned from her an appreciation of the Masters and one or two basic principles of design, for example to paint what you see, not what you think you see.

The tired Chemistry master based his tri-weekly exams. on one lesson in which he set a question, waited a few minutes then asked us if we had written down the answer to which we all replied, "Yes!'. He then wrote the answer on the blackboard and most of us copied it on our papers. This meant that when it came to School Certificate exams. many of us were given five out of a hundred for good writing on this subject. How good we were at subjects we did not like depended on how good a disciplinarian the master was. If we enjoyed the subject it did not matter much whether he was strict or not, we did well. I became good at Latin since I admired the economy of the language and was excellent at Physics because it appealed to me and the master Mr Howson happened to be very strict. He had no trouble with discipline and had a well developed talent for using sarcasm where it was needed. He would say to a boy who had misbehaved, "Do you insinuate that I should tolerate such diabolical behaviour from such an inferior phenomenon as yourself?".

The fiercest teacher was the Woodwork master. Harry Thornton,

A friend of mine who was the son of a game-keeper, stood behind him when he was explaining the art of soldering to another boy, who was holding up a sheet of tin-plate. My friend had a small, sharp axe and to the amusement of his friends he was pretending to scalp or behead the master. Unfortunately the tin-plate acted as a mirror and the offender was chased up a ladder into the timber store for summary justice. I became interested in the English language and literature but this only flourished after leaving school. I was also moderately good at French, which was useful later for reading menus and wine-labels!!

To save the masters having to carry mountains of books for marking, most work was done on separate sheets and the sheets for some reason became like currency, or tobacco in prison. Each favour required, or given, had to be paid for by a predetermined number of sheets, or as determined by bargaining and I accumulated a large number of these sheets and was able to have numerous favours done for me. I usually had my lunch in town at the Globe Restaurant in the High Street. This was more popularly known as the Coffee Tavern and of course we boys, as true disciples of Dr. Spooner, called it the 'Toffee Cavern'. When I was unable to go into town I had three runners who would collect me a meat and potato pie from Geldard's, near the Fire Station, for three clean sheets of paper. We would reach the 'Toffee Cavern' via a route which passed the backs of a long, steeply rising street of terraced houses. The back-yards of these houses were separated by a brick wall and each contained an outside toilet and a coal house and were festooned with clothes-lines. What a nuisance we must have been to the householders, running and whooping and especially on wash-days when we ploughed through the drying sheets and shirts.

Entering the Globe from High Street, the first room had a marble-topped bar, like a public house, on which were ornate water boilers and tea and coffee dispensers. In this room waitresses took orders from customers sitting at three-legged iron tables with intricate patterns. The next room was in fact a long passage and on the left was a redundant railway seat, with its back to the wall and still with the luggage rack and photographs of interesting places served by the London Midland and Scottish Railway. In front of this seat was a long table furnished with linoleum and opposite a similar table with a long, wooden bench. Thus, the further one was from the High Street, the meaner the fittings. The next room with a stone floor and wooden benches and bare, well-scrubbed tables was the kitchen and this was where schoolboys, cattle-drovers and people on hard-times were fed. This room had a door from the ginnel and leaving by this door one could go either to the High Street or towards the canal. This entrance was useful as 'down and outs' could get into the cafe without being seen entering by the front door. There was of course no service and we had to queue at a counter overlooking the range.

The menu was limited, joint with two veg. (potato was one of the vegetables) and sausage and mash or meat and potato pie: all plain but enjoyable to hungry palates. The potato pie was made in a tin about three feet square, the pastry supported on a wire mesh where it was flavoured by the rising fumes of the contents and was never soggy. The contents were removed by cutting away a corner of the pastry lid and drawing the meat and potatoes to the corner, where it could be taken out by a long-handled spoon. The puddings were predictably, rice, sago and such, but on high days and holidays treacle and jam sponge! The price for many years was, main course 6d and pudding 3d, but sadly a notice appeared one day: "Owing to complaints from Skipton Chamber of Trade we have been obliged to raise our prices from Wednesday next to main course 8d and pudding 4d."

I went to Ermysted's Grammar School totally unprepared for the sporting activities and though I was the size and weight for rugger and a jolly good sprinter my heart was not in it and I could sense the increasing disappointment of the Games master and more and more often I was sent running on Sports Days. The run took us through two small hamlets, Stirton and Thorlby, some two miles from the school. Two boys from Thorlby made life difficult for us by pelting us with wet turves from the safety of a tree overhanging the road. They took their ammunition up a ladder and pulled it up the tree after them, so we had no suitable physical reply, only verbal, which merely made them laugh. Like rugger, cricket left me totally unmoved. I was so inept that I was appointed permanent umpire. I soon learned two essentials in this task; first to be scantily clad, so as not to suffocate when festooned with all the team's unwanted sweaters and secondly never to hesitate with a decision when players shouted, "Howzat?". It did not seem to matter whether the decision was right or wrong so long as it was immediate and forceful and I was large for my years.

The only occasion when Mother allowed me to go to school on my motorcycle was on the day of the total eclipse when I was first to see the eclipse with the family and then ride on to school. The best viewing point was at Giggleswick but our family were contented to see it from nearby Barden Moor where we had a perfect sighting through pieces of glass, blackened over a candle. It was a sunny morning and the moor was alive with the activities and noises of the bird-life. It was quite eerie as darkness came on and all the birds settled down for the 'night'. I arrived at the school to gasps of envy from my companions and my ex-army belt-drive Douglas from the Great War was the star of the day and every part of it, from its fore and aft cylindered engine with open flywheel and the footboards and oxy-acetylene lighting were admired.

Occasional sorties into town were usually exciting. One small shop had a vast range of 'Joke Novelties', artificial snakes, stink bombs, itching powder and so on. One favourite was a large molar with bleeding roots. The proud owner would be nonchalantly picking his teeth and at an appropriate opportunity, with a howl of anguish, pull out the toothpick with the 'tooth' attached. Most boys of my period when experimenting with 'strong drink' tried Port, since our parents seldom had alcohol in the house except for Port at Christmas, which must have given it respectability. Many boys were cured of the habit with the dreadful hangovers after drinking too much of it in the cinema, since most of us went to the pictures in Ilkley on a Saturday night, ten or twelve packing into one of Wood's taxis and getting out in relays in case a policeman should see the mass exodus at one point.

Much time was spent talking about girls in my early teens and there was the occasional pursuit. I can still remember tentatively putting my arm round Rosie Hamilton near the gate into Winterburn's first meadow across the river from Ferryhouse, when taking her home. Shivers of what—ecstasy perhaps?

My four years at school in Skipton, either on account of the unaccustomed diversions or by reason of my lazy nature, were academically unremarkable, so in 1928 I passed on again to a new life, leaving behind my entire 'capital' with a friend, a thick pile of school paper, dog-eared with much handling but still able to make him a 'paper baron'. In return for this favour he gave me a twenty packet of B.D.V. cigarettes. Some of my intimates have occasionally accused me of exaggerating; if this is so I must blame my favourite master, a young man called Wintersgill, or was it Summersgill? When talking of some event which could quite adequately have been described as 'unpleasant' he would say, "How amazingly and revoltingly sickening!", or speaking of someone who had committed some slight misdemeanour, "What a frightfully caddish bounder he is".

After a half-hearted attempt to get me a position with the Inland Revenue and a brief flirtation with the idea of becoming a game-keeper I settled for a life working for the family firm. This was progressing from the original blacksmith's shop and small farm to include cars and carriages for hire, motor repairs, welding, wireless sets supplied, aerials erected and insurance business transacted. Later many other ramifications were introduced but it would be true to say that from 1924/1925 our business at the Smithy was mainly concerned with transport and was to provide me with an interesting future as I left school.

Chapter 6

Though we all day our work attend,
Such is our fate, we know not when 'twill end.
When evening's come, you homeward take your way;
We, till our work is done, are forced to stay.

Mary Collier; 1739.

The Smithy was a purpose-built single storey building complete with two raised tiles on the ridging to let out the smoke from the chimney fires, both stone-built, one at each end, burning 'slack' coal. The 'slack' eventually turned into coke at which point they got to welding heat. The two anvils were supported by lengths of tree-trunks let well into the stone floor and there were two stone slaking troughs and hand-operated bellows. In front of each of the four iron-framed windows was a stout oak bench with a Smithy vise and before the farm buildings at the back were built there had been two more benches and vises and there was enough work to keep them all in service. A separate door from one end of the Smithy led into the shoeing shed and a door in the wall of this part opened onto a midden and when the permanent repair garage was added in the Thirties to the rear of the Smithy, replacing the corrugated iron one my Father had built, access was made from the Smithy to the new garage.

The first attempts at organising some office arrangements were made when my Father went to the auction sale of a builder and undertaker in Ilkley and bought, amongst other things, a 'Dickensian' type desk, with a sloping top on which was a rough diary for recording orders and credit transactions. In the cupboards underneath were drawings of Middleton Sanatorium in Ilkley, on which the previous owner had been employed, and two top hats which had been part of the undertaking wear and were the cause of much merriment. Unbelievably, one drawer was used by all the

304

A.A. & R.A.C. Appointed.

Telephone - Bolton Abbey 21.

Partners:
H. W. Wood.
G. E. Wood.
J. N. Wood.
A. D. Wood.

BOLTON ABBEY,
Nr. Skipton.

Station—L.M.S., Bolton Abbey.

July 10th 1939.

Messrs. A. Lindley & Son.

Dr. to R. WOOD & SONS,

Automobile, Electrical and Agricultural Engineers.

Oxy-Acetylene Welding. Agents for The Liverpool & London & Globe Insurance Co. Ltd.
Cars for Hire. Accumulaters Re-Charged. Leading Makes of Tyres in Stock.

		£	s.	d.
	Aluminium piston complete with rings 60 thous o/s.		12	8
	Removing sump, drilling out broken studs in sump case and reassembling.		9	-
	7 studs and washers.		1	6
	1 gln. Mobiloil BB.		6	11
	£	1	10	1

E. & O.E.

staff to put money in received for sales of petrol, etc., when it became too heavy to carry in pockets. My mother emptied this drawer occasionally and kept the money to pay for loads of petrol and other purchases and gave pocket money to me and my brothers and they received wages later as they married.

No record seemed to have been made of the takings until eventually an early 'toilet roll' type of till was bought. This turned the paper roll on, each time the drawer was opened and entries were made in a narrow slot. The roll did not seem to be added or the takings checked against it in the early days. When the till roll was not taken off for some time the receiving roller became bigger and at each drawer opening the roll moved on so far that items written on got further apart. My Father and brother Jack kept records of credit sales in leather bound ledgers from which they laboriously made customers' accounts, quarterly. I gradually took over the book-keeping, which seemed a natural progression as I was the only one who went to the Grammar School. This seemed an 'open sesame' to all the least pleasant aspects of the business, like doing estimates, dealing with irate customers who thought they had been over-charged or neglected, or some other *imagined* wrong.

To help me, my lovely Mother, bless her, on her first proper holiday with Father in Redcar, went to an auction of a bankrupt office supplies firm, and bought ledgers, cash books, etc. Both parents seemed fond of auctions! Also Father and Tom Hey from Beamsley Sawmill built a wooden office in front of one of the windows. Later this was replaced by building a wall across the Smithy, having removed one stone hearth and this was furnished with bookcases and filing cabinets and a roll-top desk. At this time a modern cash register, typewriter and duplicator were installed. The casual callers who had previously stood about near the Smithy fire now found the new office more comfortable and often I had to ask them to vacate my swivel chair. One regular caller, Charlie Moon, would stand with his back to a steel cabinet, 'drumming' it with his fingers and whistling tunes which were difficult to recognize.

By the time the office was built I had engaged Arthur Coe, a Skipton accountant to help me sort out some system, as the Inland

Revenue were baffled by my attempts to provide them with accounts and had recommended that I engage an accountant. This was the best thing that could have happened, as I learned every facet of book-keeping, loose leaf and other time-saving methods. One evening, in Ferryhouse kitchen, Arthur Coe and I were poring over the accounts with miles of 'toilet roll' from the till around our feet, trying to make sense of it to prepare an Income Tax return. Cakes were being baked at the time and we were asked to 'keep an eye' on them as there really was not room for more than the two of us and the till rolls in the kitchen. We were so absorbed by what we were doing that we completely forgot the cakes we were supposed to mind until a strong smell of burning cakes reminded us! We were 'told off' in round terms!

The transition from school-boy to a full-time working member of the family firm went quite smoothly, as for some years as a schoolboy I had helped with or observed the work undertaken in all departments. I had swept up, sold petrol and paraffin at week-ends or during the evenings, done farm work and driven the taxis when I was sure the local 'bobby' was away and had worked on my own motor bike. The end of home-work made it possible for me to attend local whist-drives and dances and other local events, where I met and talked to both sexes, rather than the all male companions at school which had made life rather cloistered.

To illustrate my total involvement, it was my job to give estimates for work when required, fit the work into the timetable, which was fraught with difficulties as it was always a 'guesstimate' how long each job would take by 'divining' possible hold-ups of every description, then during rush periods I had to help with the work, prepare the account and last but not least deal with the customer when he paid the account, probably some months later.

I never minded if a customer came to the office saying, "I wonder if you have made a mistake. The job costs more than I thought . . ." as this could usually be explained or an amicable agreement reached. However, if a customer came with a bill, shouting the odds and accusing me of robbery, etc., it was a different matter. Having estimated, helped with the work, worked out the cost, made out the account, I was aware of every part of the whole transaction and never sent an account which would not bear scrutiny. The successful ploy I adopted on these occasions was to say, "You pay me what you think it should be. I have worked out the cost, knowing how much I pay the men, how much holiday pay and other perks cost, how much the firm's standing charges are, etc., but apparently you know better, by some process, so I will settle for your amount".

After a pregnant pause I would add, "Of course next time you want a job doing I want you to estimate what you will pay for it and then I can decide whether I want to do it or not".

This took the wind out of their sails and usually after some banter, the customer would say, "Right then, thee give us some good luck (discount) and I'll pay thee".

One event which tested my growing authority and capacity for coping, was an enormous explosion in the garage, which occurred whilst I was having my lunch at Ferryhouse: an enormous bang which seemed to shake the house and appeared to come from the direction of the workshop. I dashed outside and looked but there was nothing to see, however it was not long before a frantic call on the telephone summoned me to the scene. I found all the staff and customers badly shaken, all the garage windows had been blown out, a heavy car that had been over the inspection pit had been lifted sideways and had come to rest with two wheels in the pit and other vehicles and various pieces of equipment were scattered about and the buildings surrounded by onlookers who had come to see what had happened.

Apart from a few minor injuries, scratches, etc., there were no serious casualties. Bert Ward, a slightly built engineer had been near the pit at the time and had been blown right across the garage. Apart from fright and being 'winded' he was not in need of medical attention. The cause of the explosion I found was that the car that had been standing over the pit all night had a slight leak of petrol. This had evaporated into gas and when my brother, Jack, started using an oxy-acetylene cutter the sparks, as usual like a firework display, had ignited the gas. All my powers of organisation were needed to calm the situation and make the premises safe again. No police, fire-brigade, ambulances or other authorities were involved.

As my authority grew in the firm I became more and more involved with dealing with people of many different classes and backgrounds, ranging from farm men, roadmen, farmers, 'big' farmers, people who lived in the 'big' houses, gentry who stayed at the Devonshire Arms Hotel complete with chauffeur and lady's maid. I also had dealings with the aristocracy, the Duke and Duchess of Devonshire and their family who stayed at Bolton Hall for the grouse shooting and even brief encounters with royalty, in the form of King George the Fifth and Queen Mary. I had gradually become the 'dressed-up' one in authority and my brothers, much older than me were happy to do the work and leave organisation to me. Curiously, some people who were my contemporaries still call me Mr Wood, instead of Donald and when questioned on this say, "You were the boss, the 'dressed-up' one". This may have had bearing on the fact that I was the brother who was invited onto committees and acted as chairman, treasurer and school governor, etc.

All the encounters with the many different types of people who came to the Smithy together with the very varied jobs I tackled, sometimes inside and sometimes outside work, gave me a chance to develop my ability to observe life at that time from a number of angles. It was after all a wonderful time to live in such a community with its hard-working people during a period when such change was taking place.

Chapter 7

Tempus est mensura motus rerum mobilium

(Time is the measure of movement) Auctoritates Aristotelis.
A compilation of medieval propositions drawn from diverse classical and other sources. (ed. J. Hamesse, 1974).

Working in the family firm as book-keeper gave me a chance to be aware of the changes which took place in the area during the Twenties and Thirties in the transporting of people and goods. In the early Twenties many people literally carried their own burdens since not everyone kept a horse and there were relatively few vehicles in the neighbourhood. For example the farmer or farmer's wife would often walk quite a long way carrying a well-scrubbed basket filled with surplus eggs, butter or cheese to Bolton Abbey Station, then travel by train to Skipton to sell or exchange their produce for groceries or other items they were unable to produce on the farm.

There were many 'packmen' selling their wares or taking orders from their samples. Mr Denny would arrive at the local Station with a large basket full of confectionery, bread, tea-cakes, crumpets and muffins. He wore a 'mackintosh' coat, almost white with regular washing, like his basket, chewed 'twist' tobacco and took care not to spit in front of the customers by putting the 'cud' between his top teeth and lip whilst serving. He had a long round in this scattered community and returned by the 6.20pm train, having covered about six miles. He was very adept at swinging the heavy basket onto his right shoulder, helped by a leather strap fixed to the handle, which also helped to steady the load resting against his head and making his flat cap a distinctive shape. With long practice he had discovered how best to adapt his body posture and whilst walking had his right hand well up above his hip to make an extension to help to support the load on his shoulder. Fortunately for him, his load became lighter as he sold his wares, unlike the drapery 'packman'.

The draper showed his wares, hoping to get orders to be delivered later and his wares were usually carried in a large oblong of American cloth made into a neat parcel by two leather straps. At each house he would untie the straps with the pack on a floor or table and would remark on every item about its quality, size or reasonable price as he turned them over to another area of the American cloth. When this was finished and any orders had been taken he made up the parcel again, in reverse order, ready for the next call.

Another arduous job especially in bad weather was that of Postman. Arthur Holmes had for many years a 'walking round'. This meant that the terrain was unsuitable even for a bicycle, although occasionally he used his motor-cycle. It was a full day's job to cover about ten miles and many of his calls were two miles apart. One hazard was having to drink countless cups of tea and eat pasties and buns, as many of the householders pressed him to stop and would give him the 'news', since he would perhaps be the only person they would see for a week. One of the outlying farmers who suspected Arthur did not deliver the mail each day ordered a daily newspaper to be delivered by post, to make sure! There were many days during snow blizzards when his round became impossible and many days around Christmas when toasting the Season made things difficult!

The humble wheelbarrow was used more extensively before the advent of mechanisation and many smaller farmers when cleaning out the cowsheds, took the manure straight to the meadows by this method, tipping it into heaps to be spread later with manure forks. When my family installed the first petrol pump in 1924, the family dug the hole for the 500 gallon tank using picks and shovels and the wheelbarrow served to carry away the spoil.

The few fortunate people who owned bicycles pressed them into service to carry boards and ladders and a cycle fitted with a basket at the front and a rack at the back could be used for a multitude of purposes, although great ingenuity had to be used at times to ride when it was fully loaded. In Summer ice-cream was sold from specially constructed tricycles with a large box containing the ice-cream in a container surrounded by 'dry' ice. The front of the box had the legend, 'Stop me and buy one!'. Mr Herbert Royle, a well-known local artist could often be seen with his bicycle festooned with the tools of his trade; canvases, paint-boxes, brushes and easel, with spare clothing and lunch box, all precariously tied on with string and invariably it had at least one soft tyre.

A horse was obviously of tremendous value for transport or as a 'beast of burden' and through the work at the Smithy I knew most of the horses in the area. On some of the 'one horse farms' and especially where the farmer was not 'horse proud' there were some very poor specimens. Some of these were old, out of condition, ungroomed, too light for heavy work or too heavy for sustained trotting. None of these applied at Hawpike Farm where I spent a lot of time with my friend, Fred Rennard, and his parents, family and grandparents, Mr and Mrs Jeremiah Stockdale Hagar. The large size and hilly nature of the farm would have made it difficult or impossible without sound, fit horses for all purposes. The family were not only 'horse proud' but must have been good judges of horse-flesh as well. There were always three or four cart-horses, Clydesdale or Clydesdale crossed with Shires, which were always stabled in Winter. In Summer when they were out at grass they were always 'good to catch'; for armed with a scoop of provender one could walk up to them and lead them in by the forelock. They knew they were to be given a good feed and grooming, which they enjoyed and they were so much on top of their work that they seemed to anticipate it with relish.

It was a pleasure in hay-time to see a well-matched pair working well together, mowing for hours without undue sweating or signs of distress and after a few times round the field on the first day they knew as well as the driver when to stop and when to turn. As youngsters we were allowed to take the empty carts back to the field when the hay had been unloaded and what a joy it was to look down that broad, shiny back, rippling with power. They had velvet mouths due to careful breaking in and good handling and were responsive to the slightest pressure on the rope-reins, rather like a modern, high-class car with power steering. Jack was a clean-legged, black horse, used mainly for pulling a four-wheeled rulley with hurdle-sides for taking sheep, lambs, calves and pigs to market, and could trot ten miles or more without trouble. Jack could also double as a riding horse and was ridden by King George the Fifth on the local grouse moors when he was shooting as a guest of Victor, Duke of Devonshire. His favourite pony, Jock, from Sandringham, had gone lame at that time and whenever Jock was being groomed we liked to be present, since hairs from his beautiful, long, white tail were in big demand for making fly-fishing casts.

Mr Hagar had a strong, fast-stepping, sure-footed, strong pony, mother of Jack, his clean-legged black horse, to pull the Governess car, who knew his own way home from any part of the district. One night, returning home in thick fog, Mr Hagar thought he knew better than the pony and pulled on the right rein as he felt they were heading the wrong way. After a few yards the pony stopped and refused to move. Investigating with the carriage lamp, he found that they were on the edge of a steep escarpment above a stream. I recall a small vignette of life on this large farm, at Haw Pike, which now seems like a scene from the 'deep South'. I was once with Mr Hagar in his farm office about morning 'drinking' time. He pulled the bell-sash and when Flora, the maid, instantly appeared he asked for two coffees and Queen cakes, which were rich, fruit buns in the shapes of the suits of playing cards. When these came he asked for his 'turnout' (pony and trap) to be made ready and in a few minutes Roy, one of the farm men, appeared at the door with all made ready, except for the rug and seat-cushions, which were left airing by the kitchen fire until the last minute before setting off.

Most of the 'pasture looking' was done by Mr Rennard, who used a saddle horse, a long striding, light bay, clean-legged with four white socks and a white star on the forehead. The horse had a blond tail and when it got its new coat in Spring and a good grooming, no animal ever looked better. This must have been the most indispensable horse on the farm when one considers the 500 acres to be covered. Now last—and least—the Shetland pony was not only used for riding but also as a beast of burden. As boys, Fred Rennard, with whom I often stayed, and I would be roused at some unearthly hour, commonplace on farms, to go with the Shetland pony to pick up the rabbits caught during the night in snares set round the perimeter fence of the huge, disused quarry. Many times there were upwards of 50 couples which had to be disembowelled and to be made into pairs by pocket knife surgery by exposing the ham-string of one back leg and threading the other leg through the aperture. Another rabbit was similarly dealt with and then made into a pair with the first. These were taken back to the farm slung over the back of the pony and sometimes on a poor morning there was room left for us both to ride back for a large, well-earned breakfast.

Most of the necessities of life in the Twenties and early Thirties were delivered by horse-drawn vehicles as diverse as the Royal Mail cart and the large timber wagons at the other end of the scale and handled products ranging from coal to food-stuffs for humans and animals. A Mr Clarkson for many years brought the mail from Skipton in a neat dog-cart with the Royal cypher on the sides as well as on the harness. He had a smart, fast, Galloway and delivered sacks of mail to the villages of Embsay and Draughton on his way to Bolton Abbey. He then had a small 'retail' round on his way to the Alms Houses at Beamsley, where his horse was stabled for the day and he had a room with a fireplace for heating, drying wet clothes and cooking. In the afternoon he would empty letter boxes, collect sacks of mail from small post offices and return to Skipton via Halton East, a village two miles from Bolton Abbey.

Mr John Jackson Wade, Master Baker and Confectioner of 'Japonica', Halton East, had a bakehouse and shop and delivered his wares round the district from a purpose-built horse-drawn van. Whenever a batch of baking went flat or was sunk in the middle he blamed the girls he employed for 'slamming the oven door'. The van, a four wheeler, had double rear doors and was fitted with sliding trays, The driver and any companion were protected from vertical rain by the overhanging canopy, but their feet and legs were only protected by the leather covered splash-board and, in very cold weather, by a carriage rug. Motive power was supplied by 'Dolly', a neat, bay mare with no vices but a tendency to overweight and laziness. Mr Wade who was a kindly man, spoke with a lisp and was very fond of Dolly. When urging Dolly to more speed he would shake the reins on her back, using the whip would have been unthinkable,

Family group in front of the author's birth place at Dacre Banks, circa 1913. The fourth son, Robert had died when this picture was taken.

The smithy 1921. L-r: Lily, George, friend, and Father.

Family group at Ferryhouse 1930.

Hay cutting for George Demaine, with Charlie and petrol driven mower.

Father milking in field, surrounded by hens and ducks, with grandson Donald holding cow's tail.

Hay leading with Dick and father's four-wheeled rulley. Father standing, Jack with "red rover rake". Lily raking and Harry loading.

Pink cottage, old toll bar house, at junction of old A59 and B6160, now demolished.
Smithy behind with Father, Bert Ward and his motorcycle and sidecar.

Priory choir with Revd C.F. Tomlinson and four Wood "boys".

The author with his first salmon (10 pounder caught on the Teviot).

Reuben the "tramp saddler" with Dick.

Jack shoeing Jim Woodhouse's saddle horse.

Arthur Green's Timber Wagon Horses—circa 1923.

and say in a tired, resigned voice, "Come awong Dowwy, don't be so wazy!".

Reuben, the tramp saddler, used to arrive at intervals at the Smithy with a home-made cart, which consisted of a large, tin trunk on motorcycle wheels, pulled by a very small pony. The trunk was equipped with supplies of leather, thread and bees' wax and check, strong material for lining horse collars and saddles, together with all the tools of his trade. He set up in business for a few days, news of his arrival spread quickly, and he repaired the local farmers' harness with dexterity. My mother provided him with food but for some reason he liked to cook for himself on a smelly paraffin stove. He slept in the hay-loft, performed a useful service, was no trouble to anyone and went on his way to his next rendezvous with as little ceremony as he came.

The local coal-merchants, the Bradley family, delivered in a block-cart, but some of the larger farms and houses got their supplies from the railway sidings by the cart-load, thus making sure of supplies of fuel when the roads were icy or snow-bound. Groceries, often a month's supply which had been ordered from the firm's traveller, were delivered on strong, four-wheeled rulleys, in strong, well-scrubbed baskets. Greengroceries were however sold direct from the rulley and occasionally they had supplies of fresh fish, a rare treat, and a change from trout and grayling, the Wharfe's indigenous fish. One day when the greengrocer had forgotten his weights, he was seen by a customer putting his hand where the weights should have been and when his attention was drawn to this he said, "Don't worry, my hand weighs exactly a pound!'.

Butchers, who always seemed ruddy, fit men, usually drove a dog-cart and always had a very smart, fast horse and a helper to do the running and carrying. A local firm who sold animal provender had a large, powerful, clean-legged horse, rather like an over-sized Cleveland Bay, which in the hands of its hard driver never broke its stride uphill or down. Young Christopher Hagar, the son of the farmer at The Riddings, one of the largest farms on the Estate, had a neat, very fast pony and a donkey which he used singly or in tandem. Most of the day the pony was fastened to a ring near the kitchen door and he would jump on it merely to cross the yard, rather like having a bicycle leaning against the wall. He also had a miniature, working model of a timber wagon with the donkey in the shafts and the pony tracing. He used to go into the local woods, load up with fallen branches and shout the while at his two animals, with occasional oaths, as used by the grown-up timber hauliers! I suppose at the present it would require a working, scale model of a Leyland truck to compare.

At the other end of the scale from Chris Hagar's turnout and the dainty Royal Mail cart and Mr Wade's baker's van, were the real giants of the day. The usual team of two large wagons and six of the most powerful horses looked after by a team of four, huge, tough men, were master-minded, as were similar gangs all over the country, by Arthur Green of Silsden. Mr Green's timber firm felled and led so much timber from the local woods of the Estate that they had stabling near Bolton Abbey Station. When the timber wagons could not get to the fallen trees, one horse would pull them, one at a time, through the woods and in wet weather this soon formed a slimy, water-filled trough and on steep ground going downhill the tree sometimes caught up with the horse that was supposed to be pulling it. On arrival at the wagon the tree was pulled under a giant 'three legs', a tripod formed by three poles, then by means of a pair of dogs, pulley blocks and ropes, the horse lifted the tree off the ground and held it there, while another horse backed the timber wagon underneath it. It was then lowered down, the horses knowing as well as the men when to pull, hold or back. All these horses, usually Clydesdales, were huge, raw-boned animals, not as elegant as the Shire but immensely powerful. All six horses were used to pull one wagon up steep hills, which was not nearly so hazardous as going down such gradients.

Only one horse was used downhill to steer and hold back as much as possible, the brakes, large, shoe-blocks shod with rubber, were applied by a screw method, but were not very effective. On very steep hills a metal slipper was placed under a back wheel attached to the wagon by a heavy chain. This was so effective that sometimes the shaft horse had to pull. On one occasion, descending Laund brow, a very steep hill, the slipper chain broke and the loaded wagon pushed the shaft horse to the bottom of the hill, across a small bridge and part-way up another slope, then dragged it back to the bottom. Amazingly, at full gallop the horse kept its feet, manoeuvred over the bridge and came to rest without any harm.

Most of these horses, especially the younger ones, were difficult to shoe until they had done a day's work. The enormous amount of corn and 'hard keep' they were given to provide the required energy made them very frisky. When they were brought for shoeing after the day's work they sometimes went to sleep standing up. When the blacksmith lifted one hoof, they put the pressure on him instead of the ground. Once my brother George had a front hoof between his knees, nailing in the shoe, and was resisting the horse's efforts to put it down, so successfully that the horse solved the problem by taking his trouser seat between his teeth and lifting him off the ground. It kept him dangling until it thought he had learned his lesson, then dropped him, face first into the wet manure on the floor. Fortunately he was wearing mole-skin trousers and came to no real harm.

Before the Estate became mechanised by the acquisition of a Morris 'tonner' and an 'Overland Tourer', the Moon family at Bolton Abbey provided them with horse-drawn transport. They moved a diversity of things, hedge-clippings, etc., which were tipped into waste-land to form the basis of the bonfire on November 5th. Sand was brought from the river for building and luncheon boxes and cartridges to the grouse moors in August. One unpleasant job they did was to convey bodies of people who had drowned in the Strid, a dangerous, narrow gorge, to the local mortuary.

Other horse-drawn vehicles included hearses and mourning cabs, waggonettes, Victorias, phaetons, dog-carts, rulleys, blockcarts, Governess cars. These 'cars' were two-wheeled small conveyances, sometimes called a 'tub' due to their shape and were designed to carry safely small children who would have to try really hard to fall out. Entrance to the 'car' was by a step at the back, through a door with the handle on the outside. One vehicle worthy of special mention was a horse-drawn paraffin tanker which came from Skipton with 250 gallons of Pratt's 'Royal Daylight' paraffin. This was driven by a man who was always known as 'Paraffin Ike'. Pratt's were the fore-runner of the Esso Company and, had we known it, the forerunners of unbelievable changes in our lives with the onset of motive power.

Chapter 8

To travel hopefully is a better thing than to arrive, and the true success is to labour

Virginibus Puerisque (1881) 'El Dorado' Robert Louis Stevenson.

In the Twenties the local railway, the L.M.S. Ilkley to Skipton line, had been open for some forty years and was no longer a novelty. It was just part of the scenery and little used by locals except by schoolchildren and for checking watches by the trains, which were invariably on time. There were however a large number of trip trains from South Yorkshire, the North East, the Midlands and Lancashire, which brought vast numbers of people on a day outing, a typical fare being, Sheffield to Bolton Abbey return, 1/3d. The platform was about four times longer than most village stations so that the passengers could disembark at one stop. There were also extensive sidings to accommodate the trains during the day whilst waiting for the return trip. These side-lines were used by a local limestone quarry until it closed.

Many times in Summer the road from the Station to the Devonshire Arms, some three-quarters of a mile, would be absolutely full of passengers, whilst Bolton Lane to the village, a similar distance, was just as full of people from an earlier train. The record number of people arriving at Bolton Abbey Station on a holiday weekend was 44,000. Incredibly there were even more visitors in 1895. From a survey carried out from June 3rd to June 8th, 'There were 80,000 by carriage alone, not reckoning the thousands who walked or bicycled. The actual number of tourists would be 100,000'. which was quoted in the Parish magazine at that time.

In the Twenties and early Thirties, to cater for the trippers there were about 14 waggonettes, driven by local farmers when they had the time and a horse to spare, as well as several from Addingham. They stood in the Station yard and even had a guard's van without wheels for a cab-man's shelter. They plied between the Station and the 'Hole in the Wall', near the Priory, and from the 'Hole in the Wall' to the Cavendish Pavilion, a mile away, by the river. From there they also went to The Strid and worked any combination of these as well as plying for hire in reverse order to make the return trip. The wagonnettes were 13 seaters, including the driver. Two sets of five passengers sat in the back, facing each other and two sat up front with the driver. One driver when asked how many passengers he could take, always replied, "It depends on how familiar you are!".

About this time my Father bought out the Cavendish Pavilion turnouts: a bay horse, 'Dick', with a set of brown harness and a light-coloured varnished waggonette and a black mare with a set of black harness and a black open Victoria. He made the Victoria into a light four-wheeled rulley for use on the family smallholding and sold the black mare and harness to an Addingham greengrocer. We did not have the mare long enough for me to get onto first name terms with her!

W.H. Smith and Sons had a book-stall on the Station and Ernest Clarkson of Bolton Abbey, who ran a baker's business in Ilkley, told me that his first job on leaving school was as a 'boy' on the stall. To cater for the armies of people the Devonshire Arms had an extension built, known as the Refreshment Room, and there was a full- length bar, the width of the present Cavendish Room, with six sets of beer engines. In addition, many cottagers in the district provided teas and refreshments for the visitors.

Two great events of the year were the dispatch and return of the 'sheep train'. One was organised for several of the bigger farmers who sent 'clouds' of sheep to winter on the turnip fields of the Plain of York and the Wolds. The Station yard was specially equipped with sidings and pens for loading and unloading the sheep as well as cattle. It was easier to take the sheep to the turnips as in those days there was very little mechanisation for lifting the crops and transport was not very efficient. A local shepherd, Jim Metcalfe, accompanied the sheep and lived in a cabin on the field, to look after them and to move the fences when they had 'eaten up'.

The railway's fate was sealed as more omnibuses came on the scene. Chapman's ran from Grassington to Ilkley, 'Owd Bill' from Skipton and Keighley Bros. ran from Bolton Abbey to Ilkley. These were much more convenient for most people than Bolton Abbey Station, which was about half a mile from the Devonshire Arms and a mile and a half from the Priory. The Grassington bus used to pull up outside the house of one passenger and blow the horn, at which the passenger would come to the door in his shirt-sleeves with a cup of tea in his hands, indicating he would not be a minute. The railway could never compete with this kind of service and Henry Ford was mass-producing his Model T cars. Things were to change.

The first motor-car to replace the waggonettes and be used for hire including both passengers and goods carrying was the Ford Model T. This was a four or six seater at a pinch with a folding soft top, known as a 'tourer'. Henry Ford's slogan that, 'These cars can be supplied in any colour so long as it's black', must have had some truth in it since all I knew were black, with the exception of those painted at Beamsley Saw-Mill. The painter at the Saw-Mill who had been trained to paint farm-carts used quite gaudy colours and painted the wooden wheel-spokes with scrolls, lines and flourishes as he had been trained. Most of these cars had been adapted so that the rear seat could be removed and replaced by a body with side hecks, removable railings to contain the animals. However, if the owner were lazy he would leave the body, recently vacated by animals, in position and make extra passengers ride there.

The landlord of the Devonshire Arms was the first local to have a Model T Sedan. This was a two-seater saloon; the body was a tall erection, situated amidships, with the bonnet in front and a long extension at the back, called a 'trunk' or 'dickie'. The term 'trunk' was used when it contained luggage and 'dickie' when it carried passengers. Our firm was the proud owner of a 'Model T' and a cabriolet version with a glass partition between the driver and passengers and the leather top folded down when the weather was fine. The 'Model T' was the only one in the area with wire wheels at that time and for some reason a local wag decided it was a Chinese model and thus it became known.

In spite of the cabriolet top being very high, a tall person had to sit in a crouching position as the floor was also high off the ground. My brother George once took a Mr and Mrs Thompson from Barden to Morecambe and as it was a nice day they decided to have the roof down. Unfortunately Mrs Thompson was a tall lady and, to make matters worse, was wearing a hat with a magnificent erection of artificial fruits and flowers on it. This stood higher than the roof and she had to hold it on all the time. When she was tired of doing this the hood had to be closed and she had to assume a crouching position. She was determined not to take the hat off and changed the arrangement several times on the journey.

Bolton Abbey Choir and Sunday School travelled by makeshift 'charas' (coaches). These early 'charas' had side-opening doors so high from the ground that a short ladder was needed except for the agile. These excursions depended on wagons hired from Moon's Garage at Beamsley, up the Harrogate Road. Wooden seats from Beamsley Chapel were bolted to these wagons. The ride was hard and it was compounded by the fact that the vehicle had solid, rubber tyres. Later, trips were in a Fiat 'chara' hired from Park (Christian name) Stirk of nearby Addingham. This had a soft top and padded seats but the rear axle moaned so loud that conversation was virtually impossible. A favourite pastime for children on the return journey was to throw streamers out of the side and over the back when passing through towns. The multi-coloured, flapping festoons frightened the life out of any horses encountered and it delighted the children (was I one of them?) to see them rearing and bolting. This 'chara' had a seat to the right of the driver ,where there was a klaxon horn, which made a noise like a flock of demented corn-crakes and was operated for the whole journey by a series of eager operators.

Later, more sophisticated coaches were hired for these occasions, a favourite being the Leyland Lioness, because as the driver decelerated the exhaust made a noise which filled certain small boys with ecstasy as they leaned over the side for miles, getting grit in their eyes, earache or toothache so as not to miss one burst of this ravishing sound!

Trips were usually arranged for Summer as these vehicles had no form of heating and also for periods when the moon was full as the lighting was primitive, the paraffin lights only showing the presence of the vehicle but being of little help to the driver. Later, gas lighting was introduced and this was much better though erratic and messy. The gas was provided by putting calcium of carbide, rather like limestone chippings, into a dry container. Another container was full of water and, when a 'drip-feed' was turned on, the water dripped into the dry container; at which, the carbide gave off a gas which was taken by rubber tubing to the lamps. If the operator turned on too much water the excess gas blew the lights with the pressure and when the carbide was finished the container had to be cleaned out and dried thoroughly before replenishing the carbide. In the early days of electric light on cars only one light was required, at the rear. On one occasion I rode for miles with a 'Bull's Eye' flashlight in my mouth with inflated cheeks to make a red glow to replace a missing tail lamp!

And finally to motor-cycles. Many people had motor-cycle and side-car outfits which could not only carry passengers but all varieties of cargo, sheep and lambs, poultry, etc. The horse and cart were usually held in reserve, in case the vehicle broke down or would not start. Solo motor-cycles were used for business purposes. George Whittaker of Addingham, 'Boot and Clog Maker and Repairer', collected and delivered repairs in a basket strapped to the rear carrier. The Wroe family of Addingham delivered newspapers for many years on the same belt-drive Triumph. The Flints of Addingham also delivered groceries on a brand-new, very smart Ariel.

Before the advent of mains electricity and freezers, the suppliers of ice-cream in the district, Clifford Lambert of Bolton Abbey, Mrs Read and Mrs Roberts at the Cavendish Pavilion and Nathaniel Airey at Barden, had to get supplies of block ice from the Leeds Ice and Cold Storage Company to make ice-cream. These came to Bolton Abbey Station in sacks, which made it possible to lift them and to hold the label. From the Station they were picked up by the very popular motor-cycle with box side-car. This also doubled to take the ice cream to some likely area to make maximum sales.

The ice-cream was made by putting the custard, milk, egg and cream mixture into a kind of churn with an inner compartment. The outer compartment was filled with broken ice and salt petre and the whole 'churn' turned by hand, for what seemed to be an eternity. The Cavendish Pavilion had the very latest American Ice-cream Soda Fountain, which was a very large contraption, made with a delicate cast-iron frame and had large containers of highly coloured flavourings and, underneath, cylinders of gas to put in the fizz. A favourite drink was a glass of fizzing cordial with an ice-cream floating in it. On one occasion I delivered the ice-block to the Cavendish Pavilion with Dick, our First World War veteran horse, and the four-wheeled rulley. As I put the block in the usual shed, Mr Roberts asked me if I would like to take away the empty sacks from previous deliveries. Since I had been brought up never to refuse to do a job one was asked to do, I agreed. As I worked down the heap the sacks became more and more rotten and eventually were like leaf-mould. Mr Roberts insisted that if I wanted to take the good sacks I should have to take the poor ones as well and I finished up picking them up between two pieces of wood.

However there was a happy sequel to compensate. I put the sacks near to the blacksmith's shoeing shed door, thinking that they could be taken away with the manure. Later the same day Father put the nozzle of No. 4 hand-driven petrol pump into the filler of a car, but carelessly pumped No. 5 pump and sent a jet of petrol across the forecourt and road-side. My Father cautioned me to watch that no-one should drop a lighted match, but, lighting his pipe some minutes later, actually did that himself, with the expected result. It was only by having the ideal fire damping in the form of wet sacks that the fire was put out. We did not have fire extinguishers at that time as many others did not and our fortunes might have been altered if the buildings had burned down.

With the introduction of motive power in the shape of cars, 'charas', buses, motor-cycles people were more mobile in the district and despite the difficulties associated with lack of power, poor brakes, no heating system and ineffective lighting, transport of goods and people became easier. Farmers benefited as the petrol engine made life easier for them in the Twenties and early Thirties and many of them used the Smithy to have farming equipment repaired and their horses shod, then, as horses were slowly replaced by early tractors, Wood's repaired these too and made modifications to horse-drawn equipment for use by the tractors.

Chapter 9

Our farmers round, well pleased with constant gain, like other farmers flourish and complain

From the Parish Register by George Crabbe (1754-82).

The majority of farms in this district were part of the Estate and with few exceptions were fairly small, some having as few as thirty acres of 'in land' (farmable land) with those bordering the moors having rights to graze the moors with a fixed number of sheep. Each farm had a fixed number of 'gaits, and each 'gait' allowed a specific number of sheep to graze there. Prior to the Thirties, all the land was devoted to grazing and stock rearing. Later, dairy farming was introduced but before the Second World War there was virtually no arable farming.

A breeding farm provided an easier and less exacting job and was often referred to as 'stick and dog farming', meaning that that was all the farmer needed to do his job. This however was often heatedly and rightly refuted. He did not of course have the twice daily routine of milking time, nor had he the train to catch with his produce, nor to take the milk churns to the road-side to be picked up by early motor transport. One disadvantage of the breeding farm was that most of the sheep and cattle sales were over a relatively short period in Autumn and the money received had to be conserved for spending over the lean months. Woe betide any feckless persons who were tempted to have a binge while they were feeling 'flush'.

Apart from lambing and hay-time and mowing and gathering of bracken for bedding, farming was largely uneventful and followed the same pattern year by year. Regular 'pasture looking' was needed and manure leading and spreading. The manure was lead out by horse and cart and pulled from the cart with a drag on to heaps which were later spread by hand with a fork and, after weathering, harrowed by horse-drawn harrows, making the fields striped as the harrows went backwards and forwards. Sheep clipping was an annual event and the sale of wool was a mid-term bonus. Walling gaps in walls and repairing fences were continual tasks and tidying up a lot or a little depended on the attitude of the farmer or his wife.

Many farms had the typical Dales 'longhouse' with a barn and hay-mow attached at one end. Entering the barn through the double doors there was the hay-mow on one side and opening in the middle, cows tied on the other side under wooden 'baulks' with hay above. Other buildings in the yard were piggeries, stable and loose boxes for young stock. This was a very convenient arrangement in Winter because however bad the weather, the farmer had everything near at hand for fothering and milking the odd cow for house use. Water was carried to young calves and warm water added to pig food. Cows were let out daily to the yard trough for water and for a little exercise, to stretch their legs and to scratch or rub at some convenient wall or post. The installation of drinking bowls must have been a boon for the cow to have a drink at any time rather than once a day, although it often meant that they did not get the welcome exercise. Most farms had out-barns, with tying for cattle, often some way from the farm, it being easier to take the hay there rather than cart it home. This meant a daily visit for watering and fothering.

Farm buildings had been unchanged in design and layout for generations until the advent of dairy farming, the first sign being the building of cooling houses where the milk was strained and cooled by running over a metal contraption, rather like a car radiator through which cold water ran continually. Later, the buildings had to be altered to meet new regulations; the cows had to stand on concrete instead of compacted earth or clay, behind them a channel for droppings and then a raised footway for the workers. At first all milking was done by hand, a daunting task when there were thirty or so cows and the milk had to be sent on the 8.10 am train. Before milking, the cows had to have provender to eat whilst being milked; this helped to keep them quiet. The udders had to be washed and the 'kickers' had to have restraining measures taken, until they could be cured or eliminated.

When milking machines were installed, some old-timers regretted the passing of the intimacy and warmth of the old method, especially in Winter, when they had their capped head pushed into the cow's flank. Before the advent of mains electricity the power for operating the machine was provided by a petrol engine, which was usually a single-cylinder model, started by hand. What a calamity when it refused to start! These engines usually lost power so imperceptibly that they would often do the morning milking and not have enough power in the evening for need of de-carbonising and especially for the valves to be ground in. The cry then went up, "Send for Woods"! They had a habit of needing this work at Christmas and I have spent many Christmas Eves doing this work in a cold building with only paraffin or candle light. I must admit I was always plied with good fare by the grateful farmer's wife.

Other buildings were made to meet new regulations, calf holes (well named, as they were like the notorious 'Black Hole of Calcutta') almost entirely without light or ventilation. Many farmers believed that they 'did' better in these conditions of semi-darkness and with the warmth generated by the ammonia from the urine in the bedding. The first time they were let out after months in this environment to stand under open skies they behaved in the most amazing ways, sometimes with tragic results, running into walls or streams or other obstacles until they became used to living outdoors. Most farmers kept pigs and killed one or two for home supplies of bacon and hams and many side products, such as lard (made by rendering down small pieces of fat), and brawn, black pudding, trotters and other delicacies; nothing being wasted. The staple diet of many especially in Winter was bacon or ham and eggs, the latter from their own flocks of hens. Not many farmers bred pigs, except those who specialised. Most of them bought eight week old weaners, to finish off for market and home consumption. The pig breeder sold piglets at eight weeks as they had lived on the mother's milk until then and had not needed expensive, bought-in food. Pig killing time, usually in the cooler Autumn weather, was looked forward to as there was a glut of tasty food, so much so that it was distributed amongst neighbours who returned the compliment in their turn.

In the early Spring days, before the grass really started growing, one regular job was 'sticking and stoning' the fields, especially meadows, to avoid damaging the mowers and other hay-making machinery in hay-time. This work was done by anyone who could bend, from the youngest to the oldest, the debris being put into buckets or other containers in an area in an organised manner. The full containers were emptied into the cart in attendance and taken away. In spite of this being done year after year, the stones were always there, seeming to work out or be pushed out by moles, or by their rolling down a banking eroded by rabbit warrens.

With the warmer weather came sheep washing time, in a convenient stream, sometimes a deep pool being created just by building a rough dam with stones and turves or in a purpose-built place. These had a stone-built sluice with a wooden barrier and pens to hold the sheep before washing and another provided with a gently sloping ramp. A fine example of such a sheep-wash still exists at Barden on the road to Eastby, upstream of a road bridge over a stream which carries surface water from the nearby Lower Barden Reservoir. This process was distinct from 'dipping' when the sheep were immersed in water and special fluids to deter or eradicate lice and sheep scab in a specially made bath near the farm. This was usually done at the same time as a foot-bath followed by a pedicure.

When the lambs got 'nicely on their feet' they had their tails shortened for hygiene by pocket knife surgery and in cases of excessive bleeding the flow was staunched by the application of handfuls of cobwebs, these having been gathered in readiness from the underside of roofs of barns and other buildings during Spring cleaning. This was perhaps not hygienic but it was usually effective. The sheep dogs were always in attendance and 'ate' or rather 'bolted' numbers of the discarded tail ends, regurgitating the wool later.

Hay-time was a time of great activity. Many bigger farmers had one or more Irishmen to help and many of these came year after year to the same farm. They were hired in Skipton High Street, standing in clumps, usually outside a public house, all dressed in their navy-blue Sunday suits and they struck bargains with the farmers who usually hired them for a month. Towards the end of the time they came, about 1939, they could demand the enormous sum of £40 plus food and accommodation. They spent most of the Summer in this country, helping with different crops in other areas and made enough money to manage on their own small-holdings for the Winter. These men could work very long hours, doing mainly hard work and although they wore heavy, warm clothing they never seemed to sweat or be at all distressed in hot weather. In bad weather when hay-making was impossible they were employed mowing nettles and thistles with a scythe and in a year of very bad weather the month could pass with very little hay being gathered. They then demanded higher wages to stay on as they had commitments to fulfil on other farms.

Some small farmers solved their man-power problem by forming a co-operative with their neighbours for labour and the acquisition of machinery. The farmer whose grass was ready first had the first turn with the mower, but the system ran into trouble due to the vagaries of the weather. One farmer would face the Winter with barns full of sweet, fragrant, well won hay and another, mouldy stuff with all the 'goodness' knocked out of it by repeated handling in a long spell of 'catchy' weather. Ideally a farmer needed his own machinery, mowing machine, strewer and side-delivery machine which turned over the swathes to catch the sun and the wind and double up, with slight modification, for rowing up the crop for leading or making into cocks. After that, a horse-drawn rake, a block cart with shelvings and most of all, a fit young horse and one or two strong sons. With all these he could get on in good weather without help from anyone.

With the decision made to to start haytime owing to signs of a spell of good weather, the day would start about 5am before the heat of the day made mowing a hard job for the horse. This would continue until breakfast at about 8am. After a short break the horse would be yoked to the strewing or turning machine and later, if hay was ready for leading, the poor animal would have to go straight into the cart and lead hay, often until quite late. No wonder horses were not always 'good to catch' in the mornings, knowing the extent of the day's work. Dry hay was rowed up by the side-delivery machine and the horse and cart lead between the rows by a boy or girl, to leave the harder jobs for the men. Two men lifted the hay in regular sized forkfuls to the loader on the cart, who arranged them skillfully over the shelvings (extensions to both sides and rear and over the horse at the front). When the time came for the cart to move on, the person in charge of the horse shouted to the loader, "Arve! Arve!", which was the warning for him to stick tight.

The hay was held down by two crossing ropes, unless the road was very level and as these were pulled tight by one or two men, another consolidated the gain and fastened the ropes. The rope-pullers were exhorted to pull together by the rope fastener, with the command, "Heave!". With the ropes securely fastened, the load was then raked down carefully to avoid loose bits being dropped off or blown away on the way to the barn. The procedure shows how precious the crop was, as did the fact that all the edges of the field were cut with a scythe to avoid wasting the grass near the walls or hedges, which the mower could not cut. This was called 'piking' and has long been abandoned. The main job allocated to small boys was to walk continually round and round the barn as hay was being put in, to consolidate the edges.

Hay-making activities were taxing to a fit horse, but a misery to an old, unfit or lame horse left out all Winter. Such a horse, in Winter with its back to a wall for shelter, eating only what it could find, with neglected hooves, some with shoes lost off, some with shoes and overgrown hooves, would be eking out its existence. It was poor preparation for the work to come. Its long coat, mercifully provided for the Winter, looked a sorry sight with heaving flanks and with handfuls of hair scuffed off by the harness when pulling machinery on a cruel, hot day. Fortunately not many horses in this area received such treatment but there's something to be said for tractors!

Methods of making hay varied from farm to farm, influenced by the availability or otherwise of suitable machinery and because different farmers had their individual theories of how best to do it. Many of them would not allow any work to be done in the hayfield on Sundays, even if it were a season of bad or 'catchy' weather, whilst a few others regarded it as a normal, working day. Different approaches were of course called for with a light crop on a hillside farm to those required in low-lying, airless fields. Some farmers spread the hay by hand or machine as soon as it was cut, whilst others left it in swathes to dry on one side and to dry the ground between the swathes. When this was done, the swathes were turned to repeat the process of drying the other side of the swathes and the ground vacated. This was of course always subject to the right weather and the hay was later spread.

When the hay was dry but rather green it was sometimes made into heaps of various sizes, according to the whim of the farmer, to dry out further, called 'weathering out'. This also ensured less wetting if the rains came. Green hay, taken to the barn and stored in a hay-mow, could generate enormous heat, so much so that it was not unknown for it to be set on fire by self-ignition. Many times a barn wall would become so hot that it was not possible to stand near to it. In this district, the smallest heaps were called foot cocks and were made by a man using a hay rake and one foot, an expert being able to turn a row into these, hardly stopping. The next size called hubs, built with a fork often had to be spread again to dry after heavy rain, thus the saying, "Do you think it's fit to break any hubs out today?". This means, "Is the weather going to keep dry for a few hours?". The biggest and finest were called 'pikes, their proportions being like a short fat cigar. They seemed impervious to rain and could stay out until it was convenient to take them to the barn.

In windy weather, ropes were made by pulling strands of hay from the bottom of the pike, this was then wrapped round a tooth of a rapidly turned hay-rake. This rope was passed over the top and attached to a shorter rope made at the opposite side to prevent wind damage. These ropes were carefully unravelled before the hay was fed to the animals to prevent them choking. Pikes were pulled to the barn by a horse with a rope or chain placed near the bottom of the pike and they could travel quite long distances without breaking up. Loose, dry hay was swept to the barn or stack with a horse-drawn 'sweep'. This had big 'teeth' onto the ground which stuck out in front and gathered the hay as the horse moved along. The operator controlled the sweep by two handles at the back. This method became so popular that gateways were widened where necessary and bridges built over small streams with railway sleepers, etc. Later the 'sweep' or a specially designed, later model was pushed, rather than pulled, by a car converted to a forerunner of the tractor by having an extra gear-box fitted between the existing gear-box and the rear axle, to give more power. This was often defeated by the lack of grip of the driven rear wheels. The drawback was overcome by using chains or tying on sections from a wagon tyre.

The problem of getting the hay from the ground where the 'sweep' had left it, to the barn 'forking hole', through which the hay had to go, was overcome by various ingenious methods. (It had been easy when the hay was carried on high carts). Sometimes hay was forked onto an empty cart, then it was forwarded by a second man. Others invested in elevators which were driven, in the absence of electricity, by the petrol engine which powered the milking machine. This engine was then swapped over at each milking time.

On farms which had installed an electric lighting plant, usually 50 volts, or one of the early farms to get mains electricity, the elevator was run by electric motor. These early elevators of course only had to deal with loose hay and when the early bales came on the scene they could only deal with them with a struggle, one at a time. A few forward-looking farmers started making silage, in wire-netting towers, lined with tarred paper. The older farmers shook their heads and said they had heard on good authority that cattle eating silage would die rapidly, with diseases of the stomach, lungs and other parts of their anatomy.

As wheelwrights became scarcer, carts and wagons were fitted with a car, or small wagon front or rear axle, with rubber tyred wheels. One diehard, when being recommended by 'Woods' to try out this method, since the wheels of his cart were broken, said, "Nay, I've seen motor cars in a wet field with their wheels going round and round without getting anywhere and I don't want that to happen to me and my horse". When Will Moorhouse, from nearby Storiths, had a breakdown with his cart, he borrowed one from his brother-in-law, Harper Hartley, a Bolton Abbey farmer. Weeks later

Harper arrived at Will's farm with his harnessed horse as he needed his cart on his own farm, only to find Will using it.

Harper said, "I've come for my cart".

Will replied, "Can't you see I'm using it?".

"What am I supposed to do then?" Harper said crossly.

"I'll tell thee what to do." Will rejoined, "Thee borrow one, the same as I had to do!"

History does not record Harper's reply!

'Pasture looking' was and is an important, regular task on the farm and literally means, looking round the meadows as well as the pastures when the hay has been taken and the animals returned for grazing, the first point being, to check that the animals were all there. Farmers looked for sick animals, to arrange what needed to be done to them or to apply first-aid, to remove a sheep caught in a thorn bush or to take away a dead lamb. In summer weather before a dip had been invented to prevent it, many sheep became fly-blown and were soon in great distress, being eaten alive by maggots. Also when 'pasta lookin', as it is usually said, they noted any animals which were 'not quite up to the mark', so as to keep a watch on them for the next few days. Other vital tasks were to check fencing and walls, return straying animals and arrange to get rid of any neighbour's animals which had entered. Checking on the amount of grass available was important, especially in hot weather, to arrange change of pasture and one vital point was to check on the stock's water supplies.The Winter frost was a hazard. When pipes and mains froze up, a farmer with fifty cattle to water had a full-time job carting water from the nearest neighbour with a supply or extracting water from the river. Checks were also made on foxes' dens, rabbit burrows and badger setts to see if anything needed to be done to eradicate or monitor the situation. Many big farmers needed and used a saddle-horse for this job whilst those who had smaller areas to farm would walk, or ride a heavy horse bare-back, not having a saddle horse to use. 'Pasture looking' more recently has been done with tractors, Land-rovers and four-wheeler motor-cycles with balloon tyres, and it is still a very important task.

Most of the farmers kept half-bred sheep on the lower pastures and horned, Scottish sheep on the higher land and moors. A farmer with both kinds of sheep benefited by being able to sell lambs for market over a longer period, as the sheep from the valley lambed much earlier than those on the high ground. Lambs used to be castrated by open 'surgery', whereas now a tight rubber band is fixed round the scrotum to atrophy the organ, which eventually falls off. Most farmers performed the surgery for their own lambs, but a Mr Ingleby from the top of Wharfedale came to stay at Haw-Pike Farm for three days to castrate their lambs. When this was carried out all over the district, there was a glut of sweetbreads and this delicacy found its way onto the tables of cottagers and those who did not have sheep and was as welcome as the surplus products were at pig-killing time.

In the Twenties, farmers invariably kept short-horned cattle which were later replaced by Ayrshires. By the beginning of the Second World War they had almost totally been replaced by Friesians. Just after the First World War not many cows were milked commercially. This evolved gradually. Farmers would have a few milk cows to feed calves and for household purposes. Hillside farmers would breed calves to sell as 'in calf' or 'newly calven' heifers. The farmer in the lower-lying areas bred calves to replenish their own herds and for sale. Many farmers bought black 'Polls' in Spring, which came mainly from Ireland, to fatten for beef. Before the days of artificial insemination, small farmers did not keep a bull and took the cows to whichever farmer had one. It seemed immaterial what colour or breed the bull was, so long as the cow became 'in calf'. In an attempt to improve the quality of livestock, a better quality of bull was kept at one of the farms under the auspices of the Craven Tenant Farmers' Association. For many years this bull was at 'Back o' th' hill' Farm at Storiths.

Hopefully, with high Summer the hay-making was over, as was lambing and clipping time and there was time for a little relaxation before Autumn calving started. Only a very few farmers had a small acreage of ploughing and they had crops of potatoes or turnips to lift and store and sometimes a few rows of peas or beans, sprouts or beetroot. One Autumn job at most farms was cutting the bracken with a scythe or on good, level ground, with a horse-drawn mower. This was dried and carted away to store for Winter bedding. The busy farmer and his family and labourers, working outside in all weathers were used to regular, large, delicious meals served by the farmer's wife who always took a pride in the quality of her cooking, of which more should be said!

Chapter 10

O gie me the lass that has acres o' charms, O gie me the lass wi' the weel stockit farms

'Hey for a Lass wi' a Tocher' Robert Burns (1799).

Farmer's wives as well as most housewives, made most of their own food, baking at least once a week and making jams and marmalades in season as well as home-made drinks and chutney. Brawns and lard were made at pig-killing time and hams and bacon were salted or cured. William Foster, who farmed The Riddings after Richard Hagar, was in big demand for rolling bacon, which he tied very tightly with strong string. Garden produce was stored in many ways: French beans being salted down, carrots and beetroot stored in dry sand, apples stored in attics or under beds and many fruits being bottled. Baking days were high days with the smell of new, white bread and pastry made with home-produced lard which featured largely in our diets. Fruit pies were eaten in season, starting with home-forced rhubarb, then gooseberry, raspberry and lastly apple. Each time these appeared on the table for the first time in the year, each one was hailed as the very best of all fruits. Pasties enclosed jams, marmalades, currant and mint, mincemeat and every delicacy.

Marmalade making was a full-time job, during the Seville orange season. Many people cut the rind paper-thin with knives that had been sharpened like a razor and housewives vied with each other over the thinness of the peel. Drinks were made for immediate drinking, like that absolute nectar, nettle beer, served straight from a cold pantry to over-heated workers in the hay-field, or elderflower 'pop', stored for two weeks, with luck, before drinking. Elderberry wine and elderberry syrup would be made for colds and that most potent wine, rhubarb, about 100 octane if it were kept over a few years!

A typical day's breakfast would start with porridge made from oats with syrup and milk followed by home-fed bacon, almost 100% fat, with home-produced eggs, and fried, home baked bread. This was followed by toast made in front of the fire, usually a glowing, fierce fire without smoke, with home-produced butter and marmalade on the toast. Copious amounts of strong tea were drunk and very occasionally, coffee, brewed, or 'mashed', in a jug with the grounds allowed to settle and the liquid poured off the top. When there was batter left over from a previous meal, small fritters or pancakes would be fried with the bacon. Morning 'drinkings' consisted of tea and jam or apple pasties.

Weekday midday dinner was usually cold meat, boiled potatoes and vegetables, which were often available from the garden. This was often followed by rice or ground-rice pudding and on special occasions, suet puddings or jam roly-poly with Golden Syrup. Afternoon drinkings were similar to the morning.

High tea could be sliced lettuce covered with vinegar and sugar and eaten with bread and butter. If someone had been to town or the fishmonger had called, there could be kippers toasted in front of the fire. Fish and chips were much enjoyed either home-made or collected from the shop in Addingham by motor-cycle courier. Most people had a roast of beef each week and lamb or mutton mid-week. Rabbit and occasional game were welcome variations. Yorkshire pudding was a cheap food and often there were three courses of it. The first was with lemon and sugar, the second was with gravy and the third was with golden syrup. At supper there could be cold meat and pickles, bread and butter followed by home-made biscuits, although rarely these may have been bought.

Corned beef and tinned fruit were a luxury as were bought biscuits. Corned beef came from Argentina as the Infants teacher had taught us, that it was said of the Argentinians that, 'they eat what they can and can what they can't'. Eating out was a rare or very occasional happening for farmers' or cottagers' families apart from having a meal with relatives or friends, which meant that the housewife was always busy. However, the renowned Mrs Pickard of Otley provided wholesome food for farmers in the Skipton Auction Mart cafe on market days.

All foods on shopping day were put into fragile paper bags and on a wet day these disintegrated and the strawberries mixed with the sausages. If the shopper was without a basket the food probably finished up on the road or footpath, all for the want of a plastic bag! Previous generations would have been amazed with this light, transparent, strong, impervious container, which is cheap enough to throw away but taken for granted and little thought is given to it now.

Women of the area in the Twenties and Thirties mainly bought goods from travelling salesmen. To go to the shops was an occasion. Most goods, including personal and household needs, were ordered and bought from the traveller. Men could be measured up at home for suits and have them delivered, so the only reason to go to the shops was to buy shoes or boots, although some people also went to the shops for clothes.

Morland Bailey was a traveller for Stockdale and Helm, a well-known old-established firm of 'Grocers and Provision Merchants and Italian Warehousemen' in Skipton. Morland called upon his customers for their monthly order. Most of them knew him and they and their children had been known to him for years. The routine call went like this, with variations:

"Now then Mary." (Note—no surnames) "How are you going on?"

"Not so bad actually, I'm middling, I've got a touch of rheumatism. It's this wet weather. Cup of tea, coffee?"

"Thanks, I don't mind if I do". He knew it would be accompanied by a slice of fruit cake or a pasty and he had probably had six lots already, but not to worry, he was overweight already. "How's your Sally liking the Grammar School?"

"Not bad, she likes going on the train".

"How's Esther liking married life? How's her new baby?"

"Not so bad, young Enoch is a fine little chap, just like his Dad".

"Oh, that's good then. What do you think to the fighting in Spain? I read about it in the Craven Herald".

"I don't know what to make of it".

Husband enters. "Now then Morland, How's thou?"

"Not so bad Jack, How's hay-time?"

"We've t'far meadow to get in yet. Won't take long if t'weather holds up. What do you think to the weather prospects?''

There would be this and much more similar chat before Morland got down to business, all the family matters to discuss, local gossip with which Morland was well supplied.

Eventually he would get to the point: ''What can I send you this time?''

Then he would remind them with an alphabetical list, much practised: ''butter, bacon, beans, bread, cocoa, candles, dog biscuits, flour, tinned fruit, greaseproof paper, etc., etc . . .''

When it was all written down in an invoice book, Morland would eventually take his leave, to go through the same routine again and again and would return home about midnight. Next morning the orders would be assembled in the shop, weighed out where necessary and packed into cardboard cartons with incredible skill and speed. Their packing was reminiscent of a skilled dry-stone waller selecting a stone, just perfect for the gap to be filled. An amateur would have needed twice the space. Later the orders were dispatched by horse and wagon and eventually by motor vans, with the driver having to run the gauntlet of tea and gossip. After one month's credit, Morland would collect the money: ''Are you going to settle this bill?''

After a pause the housewife would say: ''I suppose I'll have to do. How much are you going to give me discount for cash? . . . It all seems very dear! . . . Go on then, knock the coppers off''. Economising was the order of the day.

Most of the houses, cottages and farmhouses on the Estate were detached and mainly delightful properties with a few small terraces and were occupied by those who worked on the Estate in one capacity or another or were widows of workmen and though many people were not well off they did not have mortgages to pay. There were many small cottages with a few acres of land, although over time these small farms were phased out and the land added to the nearest farm. All these cottages had at least a pig-stye as keeping a pig for slaughter was part of the economy.

Selecting and transporting a pig was not necessarily a simple task as I recall: when I was a boy, my Father bought a pig at Langbar, a mile away up the hill and I went with him through deep, frozen snow in the Devonshire Arms milk float we had borrowed to collect the pig. It was one of five pigs, distinguished by a black spot on one side and the building in which the pigs were housed had a false floor above the pigs on which the poultry were kept. I was dispatched into this space into about four inches of manure to bring out the required pig and each time I made a lunge at the one with the black spot I bumped the false floor above, bringing down a shower of hen manure, dust and feathers.

Eventually in this quite frightening mayhem the pigs all got so filthy that they were all the same colour. However, it was decided to take one that had escaped into the snow, which had a hard-frozen top 'skin'. The frozen surface cut the animal so it started to bleed badly and the area became like a battlefield. Eventually the pig was loaded into the milk float but unfortunately the pig netting was rotten and when it made a lunge it was able to jump over the door and escape. When it was captured and loaded once more, Father put a cord with a slip knot over its top lip round the snout, which I held all the way home, grateful to have reached home without any more trouble.

Most farmers and cottagers considered themselves lucky if they had one cold-water tap, supplying uninterrupted clear water which was inevitably fed to a stone sink. Pig food and hen food were mixed in buckets on the sink and a tinsmith-made tin bowl served for many purposes, washing up, ablutions, etc. When the kitchen fire was lighted, a ladle-can of warm water could be got from the side-boiler to make washing more pleasant, especially in cold weather. In between the infrequent immersions in the tin bath in front of the fire, people simply had a 'thorough' wash. Any splashes did not matter because the stone-flagged floor usually had no covering near the sink.

The tin bath, which usually hung on a nail near the back door was brought in for special occasions and hot water was supplied from a 'set pan'. This was mainly for boiling washing on wash-days. The pan was permanently fixed in stone or brick- work and was shaped like a pudding basin and held probably 30 gallons of water. The top rim of the pan was surrounded by a specially shaped stone and covered when not in use by a wooden lid and a fire underneath heated the water. The hot water was bucketed from the set-pan to the bath and mixed with cold many times, since up to four persons, the cleanest first, would probably use the bath in turn. The last one sat in a mixture rather like cool soup. The bath would be emptied by two strong men carrying it to the door and tipping out the contents onto the path, otherwise it was emptied by bucket. Despite the muddiness of the water, bathing in front of an open fire in the kitchen range in a cosy room was bliss.

At Ferryhouse, one solution to bathing for younger members of the family was a swim in the river with a bar of soap. Hygiene was a matter of personal choice and could be achieved despite the difficulties, although some took the easy way out and were to be avoided in hot weather. One farmer told me he had not had a bath since his mother died many years before and said, "If you change your clothes every few weeks you don't need a bath!".

I heard an old lady gossiping about her neighbour, whom she considered not up to standard and she said, "Her hands were as black as my feet!".

Wash-day for a big family was hard work. The set-pan fire was lighted in good time and the clothes were agitated in a wooden or galvanised tub, with home-made bars of soap. They were then agitated by a 'peggy stick', sometimes called a 'dolly'. This consisted of a circle of wood with three or four paddles like stool legs and had a long handle and two more handles at the top to turn it backwards and forwards. An alternative to this was a posser, which was a bell-shaped copper agitator with slits for the water and soap to come through as the operator pushed it up and down with a wooden handle. Clothes were then folded and fed through the wooden rollers of the 'mangle' and the water squeezed out by turning the handle. The water ran back down a wooden tray with a hole so that it ran back into the tub with the squeezed clothes emerging at the other side. Many housewives had to do both operations themselves, turning the handle and offering clothes to the rollers, usually while coping with small children. As with so many jobs a caller with time to spare would be invited to help. This procedure was repeated with rinsing water before the clothes were hung out in the garden or nearby garth or orchard. It was a particularly arduous day when the housewife took advantage of good, sunny breezy days to have a 'blanket' day.

Wash-days, especially wet days, when the clothes had to be dried inside, were very unpopular and were nearly always Mondays, when a cold dinner with meat left over from the Sunday roast was eaten. None of the clothes were 'drip-dry' or 'non-iron' and they had to be ironed with a flat-iron warmed in front of a bright, non-smoking, fire. The housewife would spit on the metal and gauge the heat by the sizzle. Many collars and cuffs had to be starched in a solution of starch, dissolved in water with a little 'dolly blue' for whiteness. So wash-day was an extremely busy day for the housewife. It was amazing how good-tempered they managed to keep, despite the demands on their time and energy.

Electricity would have made their work much lighter but that for the majority was a luxury of the future, since most houses did not get electricity until the 1950's. Some big houses had their own generating plants but most had to manage with paraffin lamps and candles or the light from an open fire. The wick lamps, prior to the Aladdin type with the incandescent mantle, gave only a pale, yellow light. Some lamps had their illumination doubled by a mirror reflector, but reading, especially for those with failing sight, was difficult. The upstairs was always lighted by candlelight or night-lights and the way to bed was by candlelight. The advent of Aladdin lamps and pressurised Tilley lamps improved matters although the latter were so messy to light and hissed all the time.

About the late Thirties, matters improved for many who installed Calor bottled gas for lighting and cooking, but prior to that most cooking was done on the coal fire, although a few people had Valor paraffin ovens which were heated by a large circular wick. These were made from asbestos and were efficient but smelly. Early stoves for heating pans were the Beatrice single or double-wick models and the Primus stove, a pressurised paraffin stove, was lighted with methylated spirits and pressure was created with its own built-in pump. There were two models of Primus stoves, the 'Silent' or 'Roarer', the latter living up to its name. The coal-fired oven was used for all baking and roasting and the fire for boiling and frying and needed a convenient supply of dry firewood to reach the desired temperature quickly. The housewife checked the temperature when baking and put her face near the opening to see whether the oven was hot enough.

Refrigeration and deep freezing were unknown, although in the early Thirties Wing Commander Fitton of Appletreewick had a paraffin refrigerator. At the time I saw it, it had been replaced by an electric model and relegated to an out-building. Most houses had a walk-in pantry, usually on the North West corner of the house, furnished with stone flags for keeping milk and other items cool and used for laying out hams and flitches of bacon for curing with salt. Later they were hung from the ceiling on hooks to dry. The spaces underneath the slabs were used for storing bottles and jugs of home-made drinks. Potatoes were grown or bought in large quantities since they were a cheap, bulk food. At Ferryhouse we had a box made by prisoners of war which was about three foot square, holding about four sacks of potatoes for Winter's supply. We also had a circular, purpose-built, steel, flour bin, which held many stones of flour. It was about the size of a 50 gallon drum. The inside was tin-plated and its metal lid was hinged 2/3rds across for filling from a sack of flour.

Few cottages had a bathroom and none had indoor toilets. The toilet was invariably in a purpose-built building at the bottom of the garden with a box-like structure. It had a brick front and a wooden seat with one or two bottom-sized holes, which sometimes were made to fit children. Behind the building was a door for cleaning out the pit. It was not a pleasant prospect to use the lavatory during the night and timid youngsters prevailed upon a bigger brother or sister to accompany them, or they had to use the available chamber pot in the bedroom.

Most houses and cottages had stone-flagged floors throughout the ground floor and had no damp-proof courses so dampness was a problem, especially when the weather was wet. Cleaning the floors with a bucket and scrubbing brush was an arduous task, especially if the flags were of poor stone. The bucket soon had a layer of grit on the bottom and the mopping-up rag soon became ragged. The only floor coverings were coconut matting, later replaced by sisal matting and home-made rugs made from strips of cut-up, old cloth which were pegged into 'harden', a type of sacking, sometimes using a shaped sheep's bone called a 'pricker' to poke the holes in the harden. These rugs were made on a frame of wood and were family affairs with members of the family working on different areas. They were mainly black or nay-blue as most suits and costumes were dark-coloured and good for rug- making when they were 'past it'. A border or pattern would be made from oddments of coloured material. When the rug was first put down it felt wonderful to the feet, especially bare feet. Unfortunately the springiness did not last long in a busy house.

Bedrooms were spartan, although they were sometimes furnished with home-made woollen rugs, but all had the maximum number of beds to accommodate the family. My own bedroom had a double bed in each corner with a small track between them, which was better than some bedrooms where it was necessary to walk over one bed to get to the other. Mattresses were usually filled with flock which had to be teased out each day to be comfortable but it very soon became hills and holes with romping children. The beds were just normal size but they were sometimes occupied by more than two in a double bed, sometimes sleeping 'top and tail', with heads at both ends.

Nearly all paintwork was a uniform, dull brown and doors were painted in artificial wood graining of a lighter hue. I have often wondered why they never thought of the now almost universal white. The women did all the painting and decorating with varying degrees of skill. Most ceilings were painted with whitewash, made by slaking burnt lime-stone in water. The mixture was improved by immersing the 'dolly blue' for a short time in the mixture, to make it whiter

The women nursed their families using home remedies, since doctors charged fees and medicines cost more money than many people could afford before 1948. Families were usually large and had a relatively low budget to provide for them. Besides, homeopathic wisdom was passed down from one generation to the next and often worked. Most serious ailments were cured by a 'bottle' from the doctor and pills were little used except from patent medicine sources. However, most people were reluctant to go to the doctor and would not go until home remedies had been thoroughly tried, as well as patent medicines from the chemist's shop. I have a bill from our family doctor, Dr Crabtree of Addingham, one of the kindest and most dedicated physicians. My Father insisted he must have a bill when my Mother died in 1933, a time for straightening out of accounts in families. The account read, 'Dr. W.L. Crabtree, Physician and surgeon: Professional charges for attendance, surgery and medicines, 1928 to 1933, five guineas', and this was for a household of eight people.

Pills commonly used were 'Carter's Little Liver Pills', the liver being blamed for many conditions and 'Pink Pills for Pale People'—maker unknown—were probably used for anaemia. Coughs were cured by Fenning's fever cure. Castor oil was a savage purgative and an infusion of chamomile was a foul-tasting remedy for many ailments. Overheating of the blood in Spring, with symptoms of itchiness, rashes and eruptions of boils was a common complaint and if eating copious amounts of rhubarb did not correct this, the patient had to take a home-made infusion, 'Turkey Rhubarb', a vile tasting cure. 'Overheated blood' coupled with blotchy skin called for Brimstone and Treacle, another foul-tasting preparation. Sore-throats called for the application round the neck of a bandage, worn day and night, covered with goose-grease, extracted from goose remains after Michaelmas or Christmas dinner. Scrapes and scratches were healed with Zambuk from the chemist or a home-made imitation. Many books were available which gave the ingredients and methods of making and administering home-made remedies. Often these had been passed from one generation to another.

Most babies were delivered by the village midwife, who seldom had any formal training but no doubt had an armoury of practical wisdom. Often the same woman was called in to prepare bodies for burial. Spectacles were often bought from a large selection at

Woolworth's but if those belonging to a member of the family helped one to see better, they would be used. How odd that it became frowned on and people needing spectacles had to be seen first by a doctor and then the optician prescribed the glasses and now it is a case of 'As you were'. Patent medicines and home remedies were used for animals too. Old engine oil was often used to cure ring-worm in cows. Cows were also given drenches to help evacuate the placenta after giving birth. Stockholm Tar was used to treat foot rot in sheep but most farmers had a collection of patent remedies they used on their animals.

Living on the Estate between the wars was particularly hard for women. They were kept busy cooking, cleaning, washing, preserving food and making and mending for their large families on low incomes, with none of the facilities we believe today to be essential. They made clothes, often helped with the farm chores, making and administering medicines as needed. Sometimes they managed to find time to go to Church and even occasionally to go on an outing. Visits to the agricultural shows were almost the only occasions when farmers' wives accompanied their husbands other than to Church for services, baptisms, weddings and funerals, etc., but despite the hard times there were good times and brightened by occasions, such as the shows, occasional dances and weddings, and even funerals when they could have 'a bit of a get together'. But the 'little occasions' really mattered and made life not only bearable but enjoyable, such as the family around the table on 'high days and holidays', and even the packmen and travellers calling made a difference. The rare holidays were hard work for the women, since there was the saving, the planning, the preparation for packing to be done, then there was the journey, which was often difficult due to the unreliable transport, wearing extra clothes to save luggage space, with excited children to control, but they were still enjoyable.

Chapter 11

Increased means and increased leisure are the two civilisers of man

B. Disraeli Speech at Manchester, 3.4.1872, Quoted in The Times, 4.4.1872.

Although life on the farm was mainly extremely busy from dawn until dusk for most members of the family, there were times when they could relax and enjoy themselves, for example, Autumn was a favourite time to arrange Choir, Sunday School and other trips by 'chara', train or both. A great adventure was a trip to the Annual Brass Band Contest at Belle Vue, Manchester. The local Farmers' Union arranged one year a mammoth outing by bus, train and steamer to the Kyles of Bute. This was an enormous undertaking achieved in rather less than 24 hours and talked about for years afterwards. Meetings were held in the Boyle and Petyt School, which was the only venue available, to arrange the Winter programme of whist drives, dances and fancy dress balls. The event of the year was the Farmers' Annual Ball.

This ball was famed far and wide for the excellence of the supper. Each of the farmers' wives vied with the other with their favourite savoury or sweetmeat. Mrs Willy Hartley of Storiths specialised in extremely thin ginger biscuits, which are still remembered. These biscuits became thinner and thinner until they were nearly transparent. Unfeeling youngsters put several in their mouths at one go. At the meeting to arrange this supper, one highlight awaited with baited breath was the declaration made with a great sense of timing each year, by Mr Jeremiah Stockdale Hagar: "My wife will give a ham, . . . and boil it!".

The dancers must have been made of stern stuff. The band having been engaged to play from 10pm until 2am, was persuaded by the proceeds of a 'whip round' to play for a further one or sometimes two hours. Many dances, especially The Lancers, were very energetic and many a time a team of two men and two women would dance round at such speed that the women became airborne. I am reminded of a farm-worker who was concerned that he was not making as much progress as he would have wished with his 'blooming' girl-friend. He asked a friend who was more successful in this matter if he could give him any tips. He was told to make more of a fuss of her. "Pay her a compliment every now and again". The adviser was quite concerned at the next dance to see the young lady, half-way through an energetic dance leave his friend and storm off the floor. He went to the rejected suitor to find out what had gone wrong and was told: "I did as you said and paid her a compliment".

"But what did you say to her?" his friend asked.

"I said, 'I would have thowt that a gert fat lass like thee would ha' sweated more'!".

Most farmers looked on their day at Skipton Auction Mart each Monday as their holiday, plus of course, days off to perhaps six agricultural shows, starting with the Otley Show in May and finishing with the Pateley Show in September. On market days the streets were hazardous with animal droppings as most animals, through the lack of cattle wagons and trailers, were driven to the Auction Mart and the Cattle Fairs and they were not always confined to the road and strayed onto the footpaths. Occasionally a 'crazed' bull would escape its handler or a cow would run amok and shops and banks would fill with frightened 'temporary' customers. Great confusion was caused when different herds or flocks of animals got mixed up together. The services of large numbers of professional drovers were needed to take the animals to and from the market to their new homes. These were often men who had fallen on hard times through various reasons, too fond of drink or a tendency to back slow horses. The public houses were open all day on Market Day and many of the farming fraternity on their one day out a week, became 'market fresh', a local term for the early stages of intoxication.

Characters abounded in what in retrospect appears to have been an atmosphere changed little from mediaeval times. The drovers were sometimes counted as the 'black sheep' of their families. One such was living temporarily on a local farm, sleeping in a harness room on the arrangement of 'meat for work'. He telephoned our family firm late one night for a taxi from Skipton and said he was telephoning on behalf of a well respected Dales farmer, who was well-known to my family, who wanted to be taken to Grassington, about 13 miles away. When our driver arrived at the arranged place there was no sign of the farmer, only the drover, who said, "He has done a dirty trick and got a lift with a neighbour", adding, "I might as well ride back with you for the company!".

One memorable eccentric was Bill Gelling of Skipton. All the time I knew him he wore a well-worn frock-coat and top hat, but when his coat was open it was revealed that he had no shirt, only a celluloid collar. These collars were very popular at the time. They were usually worn with a 'Union' shirt; most were white when new with vertical blue stripes and usually the collars were cleaned each night with a damp, soapy cloth, sometimes with the aid of scouring powder. Bill, thus attired, went round the town with a wooden hand-cart with deep sides and wobbly cast-iron wheels, collecting horse manure, which was readily available and which he hoped to sell to allotment holders. He also had a bucket attached to a long, wooden pole and equipped with that and his hand-cart, he would dredge coal from the canal where it had fallen in when being delivered by barge to Dewhurst's 'Sylko' Mill. The barges were moored close to the canal bank near the chutes to the storage bays, planks were put across the tow-path and the coal was conveyed in wheel-barrows. Bill volunteered with this work and in return one or two barrow loads were 'accidentally' tipped into the water for him to retrieve when the horse-barge moved on.

The farmers' wives seldom were taken to Skipton on market days so they missed the chance to see what went on.They did however occasionally go to Church with their husbands but often they were simply too busy. For example, my Mother was only able to go to Church on very special occasions and with great effort, as she was left behind to clear-up and wash-up after every breakfast, which might have included visitors, for nine or ten people. She had to wash up in a tin bowl on the large, back-breakingly low, stone sink, with often only tepid water got with a lading can from the cast iron boiler at the side of the open range. Detergents had not come onto the scene and she used hard soap that she had made from mutton fat and soda. Having cleared up after breakfast there would be a little interval before the next onslaught on what is known now as 'traditional Sunday lunch'. On our return from Church we would 'tuck in' with enthusiasm to the roast beef and wonderful Yorkshire pudding with home grown vegetables followed by rice pudding or apple pie and custard. After we had all eaten everything in sight, she would stand there surveying the wreckage with a smile and say, "Ah well, as long as you're hearty and have enjoyed it".

Occasionally people visited and stayed with relatives and some with grown-up families had a week-end at the sea-side. Morecambe or Blackpool on the West coast or Scarborough or Filey on the East coast were popular and people seldom went further. As cars became available to more people (mainly farmers) those with families able to cope with the farm work started going to Scotland or the South coast. Holidays abroad were unheard of except for the aristocracy and gentry. News of their exploits and cruises only reached us from their servants or the Sunday newspapers.

Most people stayed in 'digs', lodgings or boarding houses, the latter being a misnomer as most people provided their own food, or brought in food which the landlady cooked for them. They charged self-catering visitors for the cruet, probably sixpence per week to cover salt, pepper, vinegar, etc., which they supplied and which was the cause of much speculation and amusement. There was also a charge of probably ninepence for the use of the bath, which encouraged some customers to sneak in an extra bather. As proprietors of the only taxi business in the district we had many happy days taking locals to visit distant relatives, usually on someone's birthday. We enjoyed taking part in the celebrations as 'one of the family', as we had known one another all our lives. We all took part in village life and there were few secrets between us.

People in the Bolton Abbey area usually saved for their holidays and anything else through the Yorkshire Penny Bank, which operated from what had been the old bar in the Red Lion in Bolton Abbey, which closed down at the turn of the century. Children at the Boyle and Petyt School also saved with the bank, but their money was collected by a teacher on a Monday morning to be taken by her to the bank on Monday evening.

Preparations for the journey for those going by train or on one of the early omnibuses was relatively easy. Passengers going on special, cheap tickets were sometimes restricted in the amount of luggage they were allowed and one often saw people who had suddenly put on weight prior to the journey. They were wearing extra clothing to reduce the amount of luggage, which was uncomfortable in warm weather, but perhaps worth the saving of a few shillings.

Most people wore their Sunday suits on holiday, although the women would wear a print dress and both sexes had sensible shoes or boots. Few were able to swim and used the public baths, hiring a cubicle to undress and dress in and hiring a towel and full-length swim suit when they were at the sea-side. Paddling was a favourite diversion, the men wearing their Sunday suits and trilby hats, their boots with the laces tied together and hanging round their necks, with trousers rolled up and their socks in their pockets. Children were the only ones who relaxed and dressed more appropriately for paddling and building sand-castles.

Pubs did not provide food, but some did bread and cheese with pickled onions or pickled eggs. High tea in a cafe was a highlight when funds ran to it. Invariably this consisted of plaice and chips, never haddock or cod. Tea and bread and butter completed the meal with liberal use of the sugar bowl, salt and pepper and lashings of tomato ketchup as these were usually included in the price.

Preparations for the journey were more elaborate for those going by car. This was taken to the garage and strict instructions were given for everything to be looked at. The usual comment was: "I don't want anything to break down while we're away".

Drivers of course knew that this was a common occurrence. Were cars as unreliable now as they were then, there would be a car broken down every half-mile, with the increased numbers.

The main entertainment either on holiday or at home, was a visit to the cinema. In the late Twenties and Thirties it was a luxurious place, with a magnificent facade of American architecture, with carpeted foyer, uniformed, magnificent commissionaires and smart cafes. The film with short intervals and news-reels was repeated every two hours from 2pm to 10pm so if it was wet and one had the time, one could stay in for all the repeated programmes for the price of just a single ticket. That was sufficient time to get to know the girlfriend really well!

Chapter 12

God made them high or lowly and ordered their estate

Cecil Frances Alexander: 'All Things Bright and Beautiful'

The Duke of Devonshire's Bolton Abbey Estate has always been known as "t'Duke's" to local people, as have all its ramifications, management and staff. For example, a tenant may say to his wife: "You'd better fill some buckets of watter; t'Duke's going to turn t'watter off tomorrow. Thear's a burst in Beamsley."

This did not of course mean that the Duke of Devonshire would turn up next morning with a stop-tap key! 'T'Dukes' Estate was (and is) a big enterprise in every sense. It covers hundreds of thousands of acres of wonderful Dales countryside around Bolton Abbey, of grouse moors, hills and valleys, and includes hundreds of picturesque, listed properties in the hamlets and villages of the area, with parcels of land and woodland and isolated properties elsewhere.

The Agent, with his Clerk of Works, a trained clerk/book-keeper and an apprentice administered this great concern with perhaps a little guidance from Chatsworth. Their main concerns were the letting and management of farms, cottages and houses; the Devonshire Arms Hotel and catering premises and maintenance of all these properties. Other matters to be dealt with were the sporting rights of 'Game, Fish and Deer', as it was referred to in the accounts. In addition there was the management of the extensive woodlands:- (ornamental and commercial) rights of way, leaveways, mineral rights, etc. The maintenance of properties was a major task, involving the Clerk of Works, foremen and joiners, masons and painters and these workers and their vehicles operated from the Estate Yard, both in and around the Tithe Barn.

The woods were in the care of the Head Forester, who lived at the Strid Cottage, which is now the Montessori School. He was responsible for planting and scything round newly planted trees until they were established and cleaning up and burning after felling, with the assistance of his team of men. These men also helped the Water Bailiff (Beck Watcher) in his Winter job of controlling rabbits, as these were not only a cash crop (1/6d a couple) but wreaked havoc on young trees. New plantations were protected by fine mesh, wire netting, let well down into the ground, but gates were vulnerable points. The Head Forester had a small farm which he ran with the help of the nursery man, who also cleaned boots, guns, etc. and helped the Head Forester's wife with whitewashing, carpet beating, etc., as required.

The Head Keeper lived at a small farm, which he ran at Lower Barden Reservoir and he had the help of an 'improver', who helped with the farm work, boots, etc. The under keepers were housed strategically on the Estate and were all provided with regulation suits and stockings from W.A. & J.T. Simpson of Skipton. These suits were made of remarkable brown material, windproof, thornproof and never wore out. They would stand up on their own when taken off! For some unexplained reason, most of the keepers wore their own clothes, except in August, when they had to wear their 'uniform' for the grouse-shooting season. Fred Inman, a keeper, of Drebley, a hamlet further up the Wharfe, once told me that he was wearing his new suit, four years in arrears, which did not matter of course as the style never varied.

The year's work of trapping and shooting vermin, (proudly displayed on wire, macabre gibbets, in various stages of rot) repairing of butts and roads, patrolling for poachers, burning of heather, etc., were all preparation for the 'Glorious Twelfth'. The 'Glorious' or otherwise 'Twelfth', depending not only on their skill and dedication but also on the unknown factors of kind or suitable weather in due season. The deer ranged in the Deer Park, behind Deer Park Farm, now known as Bolton Park and Bolton Park Farm. The high railings that contained the deer have been removed. When the animals were killed off in the early Twenties, tenants of small properties as my Father were given a haunch of venison and tenants of larger properties were given a pelt in addition.

The team of joiners, masons and painters followed, year in and year out, an organised pattern of work, which seldom seemed to vary. Crises never seemed to happen in those times. Building work of any consequence was done by John Ridley and Sons of Addingham and the occasional major roof repairs, by Thornton's of Skipton and sawing was done at Beamsley Saw-Mill.

Each Summer, the Agent and Clerk of Works, usually accompanied by the tenant, looked round the properties due for their seven year cycle of repairs. They agreed the work to be done, measured up windows, etc. and the joiners made new as required in the joiner's shop during the Winter and got them glazed and painted in primer, ready for the Spring offensive. Outdoor work was started as soon as the weather was reasonable and the painters followed, usually one property behind, and the builders did their jobs to fit in with both groups. New ironwork required such as gate and door fittings, were supplied by Woods and made and supplied in advance. Paint in 't'Duke's' colours was also mixed from the raw materials on the premises.

The Agent, Mr Downs, dispensed each Saturday morning, a heaped teaspoon of grease from a seven pound tin, into empty match-boxes supplied to the joiners, which was for them to grease the end of screws, before screwing them into the wood. On wet Saturday mornings the joiners straightened bent nails for re-use on an anvil in the Tithe Barn. It seems incredible now, that the workmen doing repairs at the West End properties, only six miles away, lodged there from Monday to Saturday dinner-time!

The water supply maintenance took up much time, in spite of the fact that a new main was installed, to supply many properties, by Spencer Compton, 8th Duke of Devonshire, to celebrate Queen Victoria's Diamond Jubilee. There still remained on such a scattered estate, many sources of supply to individual properties, also the demand increased by more stringent hygiene rules and cooling of milk on the 'newfangled' dairy farms. Before the advent of this partial main, almost every house and farm had its own supply, usually from a spring, the emerging water being caught in a stone chamber, fenced against animals and piped to the house and farm-yard troughs. These springs slowed down in dry weather but rarely failed.

The water was never tested for purity and if it was clear, it was 'alright', even though the occasional foreign body or some small amphibian came through the tap. I never remember a well in this area, but recall two houses on high ground that had the water lifted by using a 'ram'. This used about eight gallons of water, which ran to waste to lift one gallon and needed a good, initial supply.

Several houses had water lifted by pumps driven by paraffin engines and when the taps would not run, someone had to go down the hill to start up the engine. Usually the water was pumped into a large tank in the roof void, with an overflow which ran onto the flags near the house door, the signal to stop the engine. Mrs Cockshott in Beamsley had this problem of the water not lifting high enough to feed the upstairs' taps and this was overcome by a permanently fixed semi-rotary pump near the kitchen door. Again this had an overflow from the storage tank. Many hours were spent pushing the handle backwards and forwards and friends and regular visitors often 'had a go' when they called. It was replaced by an electric pump, about as big as a pint pot, which was in a small cupboard in the wall: a very dull thing compared to the big, old pump.

One hard Winter the Smithy tap ran all day, with people queuing up for their turn to get water. The ornamental village fountain, which also kept running, had ingenious ducts, made from corrugated sheets, to enable vessels to be filled. Many water pipes were buried in the roads and were usually protected in Winter by thick, padded snow. The advent of salt to melt the snow made the pipes more vulnerable to freezing. The river and main tributaries did not have water extracted by farmers or householders except in extreme cases, although animals were taken to the streams when normal supplies failed.

Adapting buildings, building new ones for dairy farming and cooling houses, utensil sterilising houses, etc., created new demands on the Estate staff after generations without much change. Many of the masons were extremely skilled at dry-stone walling. Although their skill was mainly applied to repairing gaps, two considerable lengths were put up by Harry Nelson, Dick Haythornthwaite and Jim Hustwick. It is said that a mouse could not get through a wall that Jim Hustwick either made or repaired.

During the Thirties, when Joe Harrison of Gill Bottom Farm was in his 80's he told me that when he was a young man he helped to build boundary walls on the moors, which had to be thick and high enough to turn deer. Having to walk some distance to work and having to make an early start, he had to get up very early. He took with him a potato pasty and an onion pasty, both made of 'long' as opposed to 'short' pastry, and a bottle of cold tea, if there was not a stream convenient to where he was working. Arriving on site, he put each pasty on a conveniently sited 'through' and weighted them with a stone to make them secure. He then, as he put it, 'snapped a piece of each off, like a dog', as he walked past and drank when he felt like it, thus avoiding stopping for meals. When he drank from a stream he scooped water into his cupped hands and drank, giving himself a refreshing sluice at the same time. He was paid some incredibly small amount, which I forget, for each rood built, but he said he enjoyed the work.

The Estate also employed a Head Gardener, an 'improver' and an apprentice to look after the kitchen garden behind Arches Farm, near the Priory, and the flower garden at the side of Bolton Hall. Their year's work was geared to supply anything which could be grown in this part of the country as required by 't'Duke's' shooting party for about four weeks from the 12th August. The garden was surrounded by a 12 foot wall, faced and sloped to the South and had espalier fruit trees on all the walls and heated greenhouses, with a potting-shed-cum-bothy in the top corner. The paths and plots were bordered by immaculate box hedges, about 6″ wide and 8″ high and the paths were always weed free. Toward the end of the Thirties this regime ended and the garden was let to the Head Gardener as a tenant and he sold his produce to visitors from the garden of his house in Bolton Abbey, where he built a rustic, thatched building for the purpose.

The only car-parking in the area was on the road through Bolton Abbey toward Halton East from the entrance of The Beeches to Stank House gate, about 300 yards from the village green. The road was wider at that time and was administered by Skipton Rural District

Council. The first attendant, housed in a wooden 'sentry' box, was Frank Carradice, who wore a celluloid collar and a permanent smile. When he retired from the job of collecting parking fees, he ran a sweet shop about as big as two sentry boxes in Skipton and still wore the smile, but had updated the collar. He was followed by Freddy Thornton, a cheery man with one opaque eye, who was more up-to-date than Frank, coming to work on a small 'chittering' motor-cycle. How Frank travelled from his his home in Skipton I cannot recall.

This car-parking enterprise was later taken over with an enlarged area by the Estate, but meanwhile Mr Downs, the Agent, had the foresight to appreciate the possibilities of this source of revenue. He had an area to the side of the Cavendish Pavilion pitched with river gravel and put up an unobtrusive, painted notice, 'stand for 12 Motors'. The nearby sign, 'Hackney Carriages', where 'cabbies' stood to ply for hire and paid 1/6d for the privilege, did or should have seen the 'writing on the wall' as it were. A man was stationed at the end of the Cavendish Pavilion Bridge to take the tolls for these waggonette stands, for people walking up the woods or using the bridge and for many years this was done by Frank Holme. He was a local man, veteran of the First World War and with an artificial leg, which he used with great abandon, kick-starting and riding a small motor-cycle.

The Agent and his staff had overall control of all these activities, including the requisitioning of transport from the Moon family, of Arches Farm, for the many diverse jobs on the Estate. The Agent changed his saddle horse for a four-seater Overland, which was painted black.

Later this was sold to Woods when he acquired a bull-nose Morris. The Estate men were given a Morris 'tonner', a misnomer as the men said many times, "It couldn't pull a clocking hen off the nest", or "It couldn't pull the skin off a rice pudding".

In spite of this and with its Hotchkiss engine and cork clutch running in oil, it was used for many years. At the end of its time it was helped out by a six-cylinder, twenty horse-power Sunbeam Tourer; what luxury! This smart, second-hand car had its seat and floor protected against bricks, timber, buckets, etc., until the novelty wore off!

The General Office of the Estate was fitted with Dickensian stand-up desks, which were ideal for the enormous, leather-bound, account books, with the legend on the spine tooled in gilt. The clerk doing double-entry book-keeping could move more easily from one book to another from his high stool, rather than sitting in a chair. All the accounts were beautifully written in identical hand. This was achieved by all beginners having to copy onto specially lined paper, upper and lower-case letters from a text book and having time allocated to do this, as well as filling in any spare time practising. They were not allowed to write on any documents until they were reasonably proficient. Letters were written with copying ink and later typewritten with a copying ink ribbon. They were then put in a large book composed entirely of sheets of transparent paper, with a sheet between each letter. The book was then put in a press and pressed overnight. The copying ink impinged on the transparent paper and became a transparent record, complete in every respect, and could easily be read by inserting an opaque, white paper underneath it.

Wood's accounts were sent to the Estate office quarterly and came back transferred in the official 'hand' to paper that fitted the Estate filing system, with a rubber-stamped form of receipt, with a space for a penny stamp for accounts over two pounds. These were headed 'Transport, Game, Fish and Deer', Ornamental work in Woods. Repairs general, Repairs to Workmen's tools . . . Custodian, Bolton Hall, etc., our account having been analysed into these categories. A later economy drive altered this arrangement: for our account was analysed and the information written onto paper with cash columns and we had to make out new accounts with the required headings. Accounts were paid on a large cheque, headed with the Duke of Devonshire's crest and where a normal cheque says 'Pay . . .' the Estate cheques had the preamble, 'To Bertie Edward Jones. Pay . . . .' B.E. Jones being the manager of the Skipton branch of Martins Bank at the time. On reflection I think he was addressed as 'Esquire'. So that cheques made out in any month passed through the account in the same month, to avoid book-keeping 'bank reconciliations', the cheques also admonished the recipient to present the cheques to the said B.E.J. Esquire, not later than the 28th of the month.

One of these cheques got me into trouble. I was casting in my mind for an excuse to go to Skipton as I was going to a dance and wanted a hair-cut and a jar of 'Anzora Viola' a scented hair-dressing of the period. The cheque came to my rescue. I pointed out the imminence of the 28th to my Father and he said I had better go on my motor-cycle, a supercharged Dunelt, and pay in the cheque. I went to Skipton and went about my personal affairs and forgot to go to the bank. Not being able to find a further excuse on the following days, I kept the cheque in my pocket and dreaded the inevitable. Sure enough Mr Downs came into the Smithy some days later. I shot up a ladder and took refuge in the hay-loft, leaving my Father, who was amazed at my unexpected alacrity, to face the storm. Mr Downs said in a pained voice, "What has possessed you to sit on His Grace's cheque so long?"

My Father said, "Donald went in specially with it on Tuesday". Then sensing something had gone wrong, or protecting one of his brood, said, rather lamely, "It isn't always easy to get to Skipton."

To which Mr Downs replied, "Are you unaware that the Royal Mail cart operates a daily service between here and Skipton?". No doubt feeling better after delivering this unanswerable statement, he looked at his large pocket watch and said, "It wants only five minutes to the hour, I must keep an appointment at the hotel."

When he had gone, Father demanded that I should come down the ladder and give him an explanation.

There were many people around in the Twenties and Thirties who were 'characters' and lived and worked on the Estate, who are all worthy of being mentioned; many of whom are still remembered today when people get together for a local function of some kind; the legendary Jonathan Walker, of Beamsley, a handyman on the Estate, was one. Whatever title Jonathan gave to any man he always finished with 'Lad'. Thus, after having been instructed by Mr Downs, the Agent, on the correct way to address the Duke of Devonshire and his family, when Jonathan was to beat on the grouse moors one August, he made a brave attempt to get it right. Whilst he was on the moors with the grouse shooters, Duke Victor said to him, "Which is the nearest way to Broadshaw?"

Since they were about eight miles on foot from the remote farmhouse, Jonathan replied, "There isn't one my Lord God Grace, Duke Lad!"

One day when Jonathan's wife had the effrontery to ask him if he would wash up, he said, "Yes lass!" and picked up the table-cloth by each corner, complete with crockery, cutlery and food, walked out of the house with it, went onto Kex Beck Bridge and dropped the lot into the stream. It was said that his poor wife took the hint and never asked him again.

The Head Keeper, Mr Ted Larkin, whose dogs bore testimony to the efficiency of his theories on training dogs, passed on valuable advice on the subject. His dogs were always on the look-out for his commands. When he was in the pub and when they appeared to be sleeping under a bench, they always had eyes and ears cocked for his slightest movement. They never got in his way but were always a yard behind him, waiting to obey his every wish. He told me, "If you want a dog to be faithful to death, never to leave or desert you and to obey your every command, as soon as you get the dog, strap a ginger biscuit into your armpit and leave it there for two weeks and then give it to the dog to eat".

I have passed this advice to many people over the years and have never heard of a failure!

The first Friday in July and the first Friday in December were two special days for the Estate tenants, as these were the days of the twice annual Rent Audit, when six month's rent was due. It was not so much that the tenants looked forward to parting with money, fifty or so pounds for Ferryhouse, Smithy and land, in our case, as the prospect of enjoying the rent dinner. This was provided if one paid the rent before 12 noon on the set day, a rule which was often broken. Usually only two of my partners at the Smithy could attend at any one time, since we had the business to see to, so we went to the dinner in relays. The audit was held in a small sitting room at Bolton Hall, with the Agent of the day, the Agent's clerk and a representative from Martin's Bank from Skipton, the Estate's

Bankers. The bank representative was usually Billy Moorhouse, from Storiths, a local lad who did well in the banking world.

Any lady tenants were invited to stay for lunch with the audit team and they had a roast lamb lunch, followed by pudding, with a bottle of wine selected by the Agent from the Ducal cellar. The men tenants had a less formal meal in a staff room in Bolton Hall. This was a room with a stone-flagged floor, a roaring fire in Winter and benches around the well-scrubbed table which groaned with the weight of the food! The cold meal consisted of a baron of pressed, pink, pickled beef, about 14 inches in diameter, which was carved by the Head Forester, Edward Cutmore, with a knife as sharp as a razor and served in copious amounts with mashed potatoes and pickled onions, followed by home-made bread with butter and Wensleydale cheese, followed by ample supplies of drink from a nine-gallon barrel of 'John Smith's Best Bitter'. The beef, from a prize-winning steer, was always supplied by Cockshott's of Addingham, and was boiled by my sister-in law, Beatrice Wood, (formerly Haythornthwaite) in the set pan normally used for washdays.

The best dinner for the young and hearty was a July audit when the weather was ideal for hay-making, as many tenants sent cheques in advance, to avoid leaving the hay-field. At these times there was more than one could eat or drink and on these occasions, especially, some of the teetotal tenants became 'market fresh', which you will recall was a local term for the early stage of intoxication, after stock had made a good price at the auction. It was a sad day when this was discontinued and tenants were given a half a crown subsistence allowance instead.

Chapter 13

As some to Church repair, Not for the doctrine but the music there

'An Essay on Criticism': Alexander Pope (1711) 1. 347

The Estate owned the ruins of Bolton Priory, with its Nave being used as the Parish Church, which was owned by the Church of England. The Duke of Devonshire is its Patron and down the years both he and previous Dukes have been concerned with the appointment of successive Rectors. Cecil Francis Tomlinson was Rector at the Priory for the whole of the period between the wars and for many years after. He was tall, handsome and athletic, a skilled musician and singer as well as taking an active interest in botany and entomology. Above all he was as dearly loved as a Rector as he was a person. He had four sons and a daughter, Cassie, with a household which consisted of a housekeeper, a nanny for Cassie, a governess for Bob, one of his sons, at least one housemaid and a 'boots'/gardener. This handyman doubled as Verger for the Priory and no doubt was paid for by the Duke.

Servants were cheap to employ by any comparison and the reasons for their being servants were many. It was considered good training for life. They learned all the domestic skills, often caring for beautiful things in an elegant setting, so they learned to appreciate the finer things in life. Some of the many skills they mastered were cooking, laundry work, needlework, crochet, housework, care of silver and furniture, care of children, nursing and everything to prepare them for an orderly life, married or single. Sometimes the mistress would pass on items of clothing to the servants, which were of better quality than they could afford, which was one of the perks of the job. Usually in service the servants ate regularly and well, which offset some of the disadvantages of the job. The girls and women in service copied their mistresses' hair-do's and speech, taking the edge off their dialect, which equipped them to talk with assurance. All in all they benefited from this training and it was not considered a menial job. When there were not sufficient local girls, many came from the South Yorkshire or Durham mining areas and responded to adverts in 'The Lady' or other papers. Many of these girls never went back, except for visits, and married local men.

The Rector's family over a period fell on harder times and he supplemented his income by teaching Divinity at a local school and Mrs Tomlinson, his second wife, managed with a companion/help and often was helped by homeless, widowed parishioners or families that she kindly took in. Cassie, their daughter, an invalid who died young, and her brother Bob had half shares in a pet rabbit and Bob wanted to sell his half for ten shillings, but Cassie had not enough cash to buy his share. It was a problem for Solomon as the rabbit could not be cut in half. King George the Fifth was staying at Bolton Hall for the grouse shooting and with Solomon-like wisdom settled the matter by buying Bob's half and presenting it to Cassie!

A two day bazaar was held, in a huge marquee, on a site between the Boyle Room and the river in 1921 to raise money to increase the Rector's stipend. To quote from the records of the time, 'The money raised, exceeded the most sanguine expectations', and, with a donation from the Patron, the Duke of Devonshire, together with the proceeds form the sale of Glebe land at Kettlewell, the stipend was considerably improved.

The Priory organ, built by Laycock and Bannister of Crosshills, has had many rebuilds and new blowing apparatuses fitted since the hand-pump, with which it was originally fitted. The hand-pump, to be efficiently operated, obviously depended on the amount of energy of the operator and his co-operation with the organist. Although usually there were no problems, there was a story told that Jonathan Walker who called everyone 'Lad' was one Christmas morning blowing the organ in the Priory for Mrs Usher, the organist, by hand in the days before a water motor was put in to do the job. She said to Jonathan, "I shall want a lot of wind for the first hymn. I am going to play 'Christians Awake' instead of 'While Shepherds Watched'."

Jonathan remonstrated with her and said, "Nay, we've always started with 'Wild Shepherds'," and after some argument he said, "Thee play what thou likes, I am going to blow 'Wild Shepherds'!"

Priory organ rebuilds have been funded by various events. The Priory magazine of 1903 refers to a three day bazaar, opened by the Duchess of Devonshire, which raised £344-17-0d. One attraction was a Museum of antiquities, to which the Duke sent Prince Rupert's guitar, left behind by him at Bolton Hall when he slept there on the eve of a battle, probably Marston Moor. The funds raised were used for Church restoration work and for the 'water motor' to replace the hand-pump for the organ.

Let me give you an example of the water motor when it went disastrously wrong, and which we could easily see from our vantage point in the choir stalls! (In the choir, matters were properly ordered, the men and boys occupied the choir stalls, wearing robes, and the women and girls were relegated to makeshift accommodation behind them on either side of the Chancel, and until fairly recently they were not provided with robes). The water motor chose an inopportune time to misbehave. One Sunday in August, when King George the Fifth and Duke Victor were attending Evensong, a pipe burst and a jet of water went over the vestry screen and sprayed these unfortunate gentlemen! I was fascinated to see what they would do. They were for me (a boy at the time) the two top men in the universe. Duke Victor, the 9th Duke of Devonshire, owned everything in sight. Everyone I knew were his workmen or tenants and the King was the ruler of about half the world, according to the pink areas on the school map. The anti-climax, the least expected thing I thought would happen, did: they merely moved back a few pews.

In 1926, a further rebuild and the provision of the paraffin engine blower was financed by a two day bazaar, held in a huge marquee between the Boyle Room and the River, and followed the usual fund-raising pattern of concerts, dancing to Skipton Band, 'bran tubs', farcical sketches and stalls of every description. The same year, a fancy-dress ball was held in the Boyle and Petyt School, which helped with the profit, a further £4-18-3d. The organ re-build, in 1926/27 included a pneumatic action, powered by a paraffin engine, which was installed in an underground chamber in the grave-yard. The chamber however was not water tight and from the outset water had to be lifted from a settlement pit by two men or lads with a bucket and rope, which provided many opportunities for larks! Later a semi-rotary pump was permanently fitted to the wall, half-way down the iron ladder, made by Woods. Huge fans were in the underground chamber and wind was delivered through the Priory wall in a large, leather sleeve. One particularly wet day, when the pump could hardly keep pace with the water entering, we decided to see what would happen if the water level reached the fans. The organist nearly fell off his stool when he started playing an 'involuntary' of water music!

On occasions when the engine stopped, the organ, as it became short of air, did a glissando into a high-pitched, obscure key. Should the trouble be only a hiccup, such as a plug not firing for a few revolutions and then recovering, there was a glissando upwards, followed by a glissando downwards. Once, while I was still at Ermysted's, when we knew one of our contemporaries was to sing a solo, we listened at the North-West door for him to get under-way and then introduced two short periods of misfire, giving the poor unfortunate two double, disconcerting glissandos! Discipline in the choir however was very strict and talking was strictly forbidden in the vestry, before and after the service. Any boys who misbehaved during the service got a quick jab with Ancient and Modern from the man behind. At that time the shelf for books was ideally placed for these reminders to be administered.

Recalling these events reminds me, that my friends and I had a bit of fun one dark, Autumn evening after choir practice. The Rector asked us to take our surplices home to be washed for the wedding of a choir member. The choirboys hit on a plan to terrorise the Duke's agent, who was also 'Rector's Warden'. He was a man of habit and always went for a walk down Bolton Lane at 9pm. We arranged to converge silently on him, on our bicycles with the oil lamps extinguished, at a 'spooky' point near a hollow tree. We had all in the past been scared there by our mates and we planned to wear our surplices and make ghostly noises. We were sure Mr Downs would flee in terror however, he said, "You stupid donkeys, you will tear your surplices. Wait until I see the Rector!"

If I have given the impression that all we thought about was practical jokes or japes of one kind or another, that would not be true. The messages of the various seasons of Church life did affect us and our behaviour. The Lenten and Passiontide services and hymns, culminating in the singing of Stainer's 'Crucifixion' on Good Friday, or some similar work, moved us deeply, with a real sense of grief and our behaviour was always more restrained. Similarly we had a real feeling of elation on Easter Day as we processed, as on other special days, the long way round, from the original vestry, adjacent to the organ, via the North aisle and up the centre aisle to the choir stalls.

The message of Whitsuntide was rather overshadowed by the 'fashion parade', as most of the women and girls turned up in their new finery, which each of them had kept as a jealously guarded secret until Whitsunday. There was mutual admiration and 'Oos's' and 'Ah's' were bandied about. When the congregation was seated, there was the opportunity for a closer appraisal of style, cut and material, not forgetting the millinery, all of which were a distraction from the Whitsuntide message, of the coming of the Holy Ghost. Christmas had, of course, its usual magic for all of us. Nothing, for me, can transcend the memory of the Christmas Eve carol service by the light of candles and the paraffin lamps, with all our neighbours and family round us, with Willy Hartley, from Storiths, taking the part of Good King Wenceslas and the nervous, young, Donald Wood his 'page'.

In the late Twenties and early Thirties, as a young man, I became involved occasionally in 'officiating' in the 'said' Service of Evensong at Beamsley Alms Houses (Beamsley Hospital). The Hospital was owned and administered by Skipton Castle Estate and there were 13 separate, mainly one-roomed dwellings at that time, reserved for widows of work people employed by that estate. On either side of the entrance archway were three rooms, with three outside lavatories and coal houses. The circular building at the top of the path contained seven dwellings, each with one room, with the exception of the 'Mother's', which had two rooms. These seven rooms were built round a circular Chapel with a pulpit and pews.

Above the Chapel there was a circular, lantern tower and a belfry.

These women were obliged, when they were fit, to attend Evensong on Sundays and Wednesday afternoons. The services were usually taken by the Rector of the Priory and in his absence by Mr Soar, the butler from Farfield Hall and when he went abroad with his employer, Mr George Douglas, I was called in as deputy's deputy. I went to the Hospital on my ex-War Department, belt-driven Douglas in its camouflaged livery, wearing plus-fours, this being the fashion, or sand-coloured Oxford bags, at their most extreme, with about 34″ diameter legs. On one occasion, emerging from the 'Mother's' spare room where I had donned my surplice, I heard one of the old residents say in a loud voice,

"I've niver seen a parson before in a get-up like that!"

At that time there was no organ in the Chapel and I found it difficult to select a starting note for the first hymn so, before I used to set out to conduct a Service there, I would get the note on the piano at home and hum it all the way to the Alms Houses while riding my motor-cycle. When I was changing into my surplice I would hum the note, to keep it in my head. One time, the note I had tried to retain had moved up the scale somewhat, so that when the hymn started it was quite obvious, after a line or two, that none of us could stand the pace. One of the residents, as the singing became quieter through lack of people joining in, said, "Nay, Lad, Thou'll hev to start lower down."

On one occasion one of them showed me a box in a chest of drawers, containing some silver spoons and said, "When thou hears I've snuffed it, thee come up and get these spoons. I don't want them vultures to get 'em."

The 'vultures', whoever they were, would get them because I could not see how I could get them without infringing the Law. On safer ground there were such tasks as getting in coal when it was icy or even removing the tight lid off a pot of marmalade or jam. They always had jobs waiting for me to do, whenever I 'officiated' at any of their services. But life in the Hospital, sheltered as it was, would never have been the same for them as it would have been in their own cottages or farms.

Chapter 14

Our democracy was from an early period, the most aristocratic, and our aristocracy the most democratic in the world

'History of England' Vol. 1 (1849) Ch.1 Thomas Babington,
1st Baron Macaulay.

Duke Victor was the owner of the Bolton Abbey Estate, although in the name of the Chatsworth Estates Company for some of the time. He also owned other estates in Derbyshire, Scotland and Ireland and considerable property in Eastbourne and London. He made annual visits to Bolton Abbey for the grouse shooting, accompanied by the Duchess and his large family and friends, who became well known, not only by the staff and game-keepers, but also by many of the workmen, farmers and farmers' sons who helped on the shoot.

Most house parties included some or all of the Duke's daughters, Ladies Maud, Blanche, Dorothy, Rachel and Anne, their husbands and their children. Bolton Hall would overflow so much that the nursery (small children, nannies and nursemaids) had to be housed, for many years, at Arches Farm. The Duchess and Marchioness would visit houses and cottages on the Estate, especially where there was sickness or bereavement. and were often accompanied by daughters and granddaughters.

The Hall, where the house parties were held, was lighted by paraffin lamps during the Twenties and early Thirties and the Lamp Room referred to where 'Old Ben', the lamp man from Chatsworth trimmed and cleaned the lamps each day, a full-time job. There were lamps of every description and size, ornate ones for the Hall with beautiful shades and bowls and plain ones with polished reflectors for all the passages. He thought it was terrible when the lamps were converted to use electricity when mains electricity came to the Hall. Woods delivered most days ten gallons of best paraffin and I was often entertained by Ben's stories of Chatsworth, in what he called

Early sign when Father and George were sole partners.

Father with Dick and waggonette. Jack about to shoe pony, and onlookers.

Harry and Beatrice in Ford Model 1 with wire wheels and father.

Camping holiday with two good friends, George Demaine and ''Beetle''.

Austin 20 taxi, about to leave Beamsley school with Barden children. Picture circa early 1930's includes some onlookers.

George and Donald with consignment of ironwork (including hand-made nails) ready for despatch to St John's Church Pinner.

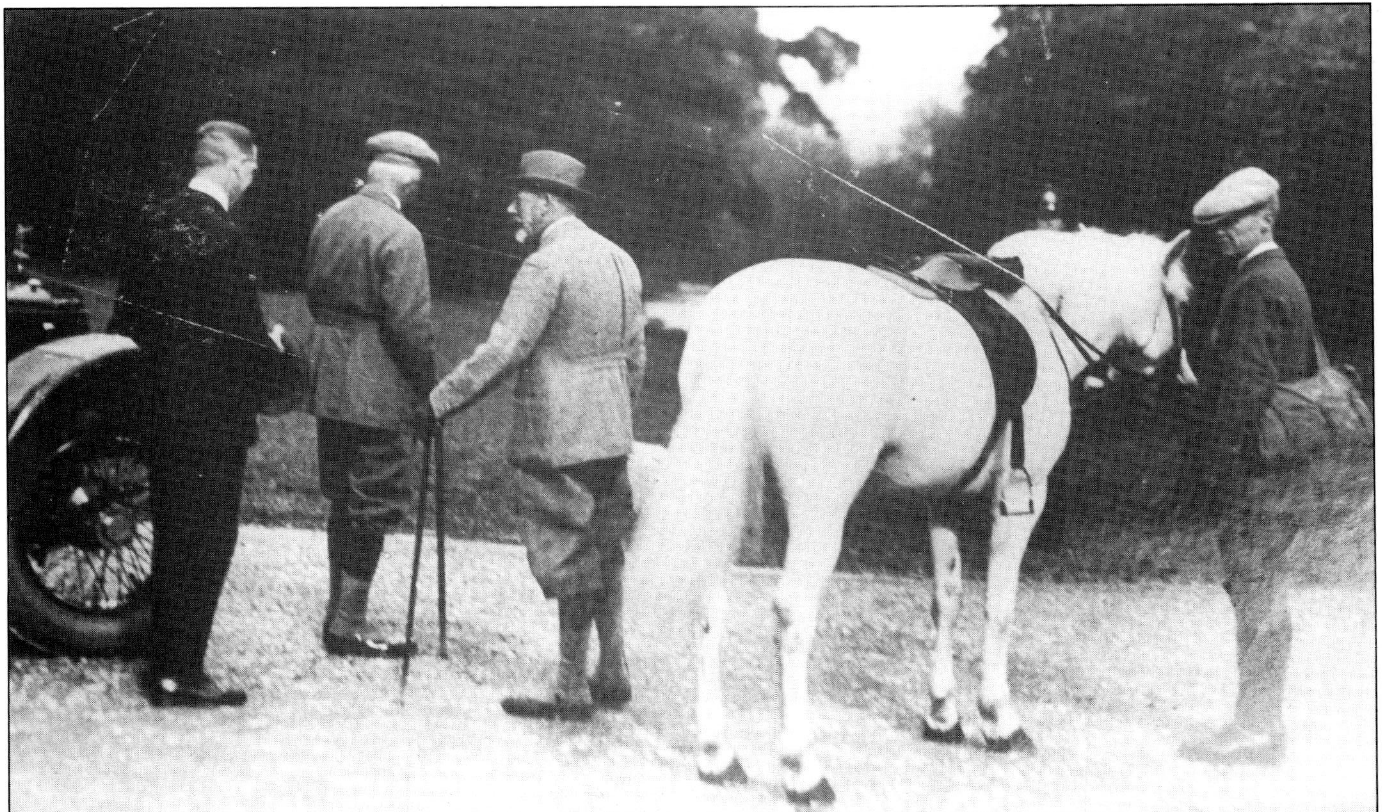

King George V and Victor IXth Duke of Devonshire, with Jock and the King's chauffeur and ponyman, watched by London "Bobby".

Smithy blackboard, author making note of dental appointment, drawings of ironworks and illustration of joke from "Punch".

Yesterday (seated).

Today addressing Wharfedale Piscatorials.

The author proudly adds another brand to a well branded door.

‘the good old days’. It is strange how the halcyon days are always years and years ago, by which token although I did not realise it, I was going through my ‘good old days’ when I was talking with Ben.

Each year on one day during their stay, a cricket team came from Chatsworth to play the local team, preceded by a luncheon at the Devonshire Arms Hotel. The return match was another highlight in the calendar. Those who did not meet ‘the Family’ on such occasions met them on special days when tenants, workmen and their wives from the Bolton Abbey Estate and a number of other people went to Chatsworth for ‘coming of age’ parties, weddings, etc., which were always memorable occasions. They still continue. The present Duke, Andrew, the 11th Duke of Devonshire, has recently splendidly celebrated the Tercentenary of the Dukedom at Chatsworth and all the tenants from the Bolton Abbey Estate were invited, as were tenants from his other Estates.

I drove Mr Downs, the Agent, to a wedding at Chatsworth as he was unfit to drive such a long distance. As I watched the arrival of the Duke’s 40/50 Rolls Royce with footman and chauffeur, with gold stringing and crest I was able to compare them with the American cars owned by some of the guests. The Rolls made no noise other than that caused by the wheels on the gravel. As John Betjeman said in his poem, ‘Indoor Games at Newbury’: ‘Short is the way your chauffeurs travel, crunching over private gravel’. The American cars in contrast seemed noisy, had acres of chrome-plate, enormous bumpers, with over-riders on the over-riders, white-walled tyres and the exaggerated bulbous bodies of the period.

The reception for the wedding at ‘The House’ was in two large rooms, each with a long table, groaning with food and there was a constant report of champagne corks, like machine-gun fire. Land-owners and lorry drivers, bishops and blacksmiths all rubbed shoulders good-naturedly. When they had all eaten and drunk their fill, it was announced that the bride and bride-groom were about to leave by the West door and most people went to see them off. I remained behind, wondering if I could force myself to have one other delicacy, not having gone through the complete ‘card’. When the room cleared, a side door was opened and all the children from

Chatsworth swooped in and like a swarm of locusts, cleared every item from the first table, becoming more selective as they went further down and finally had to admit defeat.

At a much later wedding I attended when the present Marquess of Hartington was a small boy, he took a fancy to beating the gold trays which were standing on a shelf. The caterers came from London on that occasion and one waiter becoming tired of the din got hold of the Marquess by his ankle and said in no uncertain manner, "Push off, you blinking perisher".

The youthful drummer was not deterred and started up again, some distance away! So life on the Estate was varied and enjoyable even if sometimes there never seemed to be enough hours in the day to do what needed to be done. This especially applied when 'the Family' was up for grouse shooting and involved a tremendous amount of organisation to make it an enjoyable time for the Duke's family and guests.

Mention the Estate, and people have an image of the Priory, the Cavendish Pavilion, Barden Tower (a local, picturesque ruin) but most of all they talk of the scenery, the woods, the winding river and the hills but walkers talk of the wildness of the moor-tops, the grouse calling and the ever-changing distant views. The Estate covers 30,000 acres, while about 1,500 acres are forested. Nearly half the Estate is farmland, mainly marginal upland farming, but there is some good dairy land. Scattered hamlets, farms and occasional small villages dot the area, according with the landscape. The remainder is mainly moorland, purple, grey or brown according to the season, with outcrops of rock. Here in the weather-beaten moor-tops the grouse flies low, disturbed by your approach, calling 'go back, go back, go back!'.

The keepers' main objective was to provide excellent sport for the Duke, his family and guests when they came up from Chatsworth each August. They helped to do this by patch-burning the heather to provide a good environment for grouse to flourish and by keeping down predators, which included poachers. The few weeks when 'the Family' were in residence at Bolton Hall was for many the highlight of the year, with most of the Estate workers, local farmers, their sons and schoolboys being employed with the Shoot. Many helpers were needed, as beaters, flankers, cartridge carriers, loaders, 'bird-huggers', pony men and dog-handlers. For all it was hard work, involving walking long-distances over rough terrain, sometimes made worse by rain, high winds or hot sun. Everybody enjoyed the change from their normal routine. It was of course the only time in the year when many of the boys and men of the village were all together and much reminiscing went on about previous years.

A typical day's shooting at that time would usually go as follows: the first off would probably be the lunch cart, especially if the lunch cabin was one of the more distant ones. A block cart pulled by one horse, loaded with lunches, cartridges for the later drives and drinks for the whole party and helpers was usually in the charge of Mr Harry Moon and he had one or two footmen with him. The next off would be the beaters who were taken as far as practicable by motor transport, from which point they set off on foot for many miles to form a large half-circle across the moor. Their task was, on the signal of two rapid shots by Duke Victor, to converge on the first set of butts, waving flags and shouting some traditional form of gibberish, which I never really mastered, to drive the birds towards the guns.

Soon after, the ponies, some from local farms, some from Chatsworth and when King George the Fifth was a guest, Jock, the much painted and photographed pony from Sandringham, would all be ridden or led. There were usually six pony-men taking twelve ponies to the point where the 'Guns' would alight from their cars. Later, the loaders, cartridge-carriers, flankers, keepers, etc., collected in the Gun Room at Bolton Hall, complete with about twelve dogs, mainly Labradors, all unbelievably well-trained and obedient and were driven to their rendezvous in the magnificent, new, Albion brake, driven by the young Irish chauffeur who later, and for many years, became the present Duke's driver. The last away would be the 'Guns', having determined the number of the butt they would occupy by drawing 'straws' from an ingenious gold device, rather like a miniature umbrella, which was twirled round and on pushing a slide the spokes came out, rather like an umbrella turned inside out by the wind. Each spoke had a number between one and twelve. This number for the butt was not allocated for the whole day and in true sporting manner each 'Gun' moved up two after each drive, so that it was a matter of luck who got the advantage or otherwise of the wind or a low sun.

When everyone had arrived at the predetermined place on the moor, from which the only way forward was on foot or pony, the small army set off, led by the Head Keeper, the Duke and his eleven guests on twelve ponies, followed by the pony men, twelve loaders with twenty-four guns, twelve cartridge-carriers, two bird- huggers, fifteen dogs, the pannier horse with attendant, the bird cart and driver, as well as assorted flankers, keepers, etc. There would be about seventy-eight men and animals who were involved in the Shoot.

Fred Inman who was a keeper and helped me with bird-hugging was one of the nicest men I have ever met. He was almost crippled with rheumatism or arthritis, never complained or grumbled and taught me how to walk on rough going. He said, "Always decide before you move your foot where you are going to put it down, mark the spot in your mind and do it every time, no matter how tedious it may seem at first".

What a difference it made, much less jarring or tiring, since prodigious numbers of miles were covered on a Shoot.

The return journey would be swelled by about a further ten ladies and children who usually joined the party at lunch-time, the ponies being sent during the last drive before lunch to pick them up. Of course when the King was shooting the numbers of people increased enormously, by Equerries, detectives and 'plain-clothes' police and I was proud both as a boy and as a young man to be a part of this pageant.

One hot, Summer day I was sitting on a bed of bilberry waiting for the 'off', no activity was expected until Duke Victor gave the signal and my attention was drawn to the insect life all around me. On that square yard was a complete sermon on the Creation and about humility. It was just one small area, like countless millions more. I was reminded of the Psalmist, who wrote of 'Creeping things innumerable', all going about their business, carrying and fetching, feeding, etc. and big as I was by comparison, I was of no concern to them.

When Duke Victor gave the signal for the 'off', the beaters would start to converge on the butts, with their traditional commotion, with the 'Guns' at the ready, standing in the butts, waiting for the birds to break cover. Their loaders would stand near them, ready to re-load quickly and pass the second gun to the shooter, ready loaded. The cartridge-carrier would sit in the butt to mark the spot where any birds fell behind the butts. Some 'Guns' would use magnificent, matched 'Purdeys'. The birds would break cover and fly over the butts, with the 'Guns' shooting as many as they were able before they passed overhead. The bird-huggers would act as flankers to drive any stray birds toward the butts. When the drive was over the shot birds would be collected by the cartridge-carriers, 'Guns', loaders and dogs and the bird-huggers would pick up the empty cartridge cases from the butts to be taken away with the birds. All the birds would then be placed into neat rows and counted and a bird-hugger would mark the game-card for each 'Gun'. The birds would then be taken to the pannier horse, for many years in the charge of Fred Parkinson from Hazelwood who took them to the game cart, a four-wheeled rulley with hampers, driven by Bert Croft of Noska. When the drive was over the beaters formed a semi-circle round another area of moorland and the 'Guns', loaders, cartridge-carriers and dogs moved off to the next row of butts and the whole procedure would start again.

In a lull during one drive, when I was acting as cartridge-carrier, Duke Victor asked my name and when I said it was Wood he seemed enormously amused. I did not realise why until his loader Jack Stone winked at me as the Duke said, "Good God, I have two men, one made of wood and one of stone!"

I learned one valuable lesson from Jack. He was indeed a man of stone and totally ignored the weather, standing full-face into whatever came at him, wearing only his keeper's suit, which was the type used at Chatsworth and had a storm tab on the left lapel to fasten to a button behind the right lapel, which was useful in cold, wind or rain. Jack told me, "It's no help to make a fuss about the weather, blowing or muttering does not help in the slightest".

When King George the Fifth was a member of the shoot I was cartridge-carrier to his Equerry, Sir Charles Cust, and as he was always in the next butt to His Majesty I had many opportunities to observe the King at close quarters. He was a remarkable shot. Once he brought down a brace of snipe, one with each barrel. His matched pair of Purdeys', although hammerless had dummy hammers, so that after years of using hammer guns he was able to get a better 'bead' on the birds. His bag was sometimes swollen by birds brought in by keepers picking up a spare bird and taking it to his butt to take a closer look at him and remarking, "One of yours I think, your Majesty".

The cartridge cases used by the King were in much demand for souvenirs or for reloading, since they were made of brass.

When the ladies arrived for luncheon to join the 'Guns' they would eat in one luncheon cabin with them and were joined by the children and their nannies, while those assisting with the Shoot ate in another. I remember lunching at 'North Pole Cabin' and looking down onto what I now know is the Burnsall/Rylstone area and seeing it from this unusual standpoint I thought it must be somewhere in the Lake District, in view of the distance we had walked to get where we were.

The Estate workers would bring their own sandwiches but receive a bottle of 'Schweppes Ginger Beer' which had been brought on the luncheon cart. Ninepence was deducted from the day's pay of nine shillings for the drink, however when payment was made for the fifteen to twenty days' work, it was a sizable sum. It was enough for me at one time to have bought a new bicycle with dropped handlebars and dynamo lighting, with money to spare. The ginger beer was a fiery, unsuitable drink for our palates. As a boy, and on behalf of the other boys, I had the temerity to ask if it could be replaced by a 'monster' bottle of lemonade or 'Dandelion and Burdock' from the local Mineral Water Factory at Addingham. This was refused on the grounds that it would overload the lunch cart. However, to offset that set-back, there was an occasion when a dog stole my packed lunch and Sir Charles Cust, hearing of my misfortune, sent a footman with food from the Royal table!

I shall always remember those outings with pleasure and delight to recall meeting the 'wit and nobility' under those circumstances. It was marvellous to be on a Shoot with King George the Fifth present, at a time when the British Commonwealth was flourishing and he seemed to me to be so powerful. Some of Duke Victor's family who usually came up for the grouse shooting were headed for high office. Duke Victor had already been Governor General of Canada, where his Aide was Mr Harold MacMillan, who later became Prime Minister and frequently shot with the Duke. He had married Lady Dorothy Cavendish, one of the Duke's daughters. Others who regularly came up for the 'Glorious Twelfth' were the Duke's elder son, Edward, Marquess of Hartington and his two sons, William, Earl of Burlington, and Lord Andrew, Lord Charles Cavendish was also a regular 'Gun'. Captain Bailey, Mr Ivan Cobbold, Captain Stuart and Mr Henry Hunloke were Duke Victor's sons-in-law and regular 'Guns'. Another relative of the Marquess and Marchioness who was a regular visitor and guest at Bolton Abbey for the shoots and as a visitor was The Right Hon. David Ormsby-Gore, who later, as Lord Harlech, became our Washington Ambassador. With our contact with all these public figures, had we but realised it, what opportunities for name-dropping might have lain in store!

I was glad that I got to know vast areas of my native heath the hard way, on foot. They were areas I would not have seen had I not spent so much time with the shooting parties. It has been good to be able in later life to talk intelligently and with interest with keepers and beaters and 'Guns' of details of 'bags' and incidents: talk of 'Brass Castle', 'Old Wife's Crag', 'Deer Gallows', 'Scale Bents' and so on, which were all names of drives or luncheon cabins. Remembering this former life has brought me great pleasure and reminded me of drinking that absolute nectar, the crystal-clear, icy water issuing from a spring near Spring Brow, on a boiling hot day and getting to know King George the Fifth's exquisite, gentle pony, Jock. I still have a non-flashing fly-fishing cast made from his long, white tail, which was invaluable before the days of nylon. Happy days!

Chapter 15

Sport that wrinkled Care derides. And Laughter holding both his sides...

L'Allegro (1695) 1.1. John Milton

The Estate fishing extended some five miles on both banks, from below Bolton Bridge to Barden Bridge and this was reserved for the Duke's family and his Agent, but principally for the residents at the Devonshire Arms. The 'bag' limit between the wars was twenty fish, not less than eight inches. A good, well fed trout weighed half a pound at that length and is still in my opinion the ideal size for a Wharfe, wild, brown trout. Before the advent of extensive land and moor drainage the river rose and ran off more slowly, so much so that when it was in good fishing order the proprietors of the Devonshire Arms used to send telegrams to their fishing clients. This meant that they were able to arrange their affairs and come by taxi or by car for the sport.

Thomas Reid, who lived at the hotel for years, fished every day of the season and went to fish in Dovedale in Derbyshire for his holidays, staying at the famous Izaak Walton Hotel. He was always immaculate, dressed every evening for dinner, wore hand-made boots, had his suits made in Saville Row and went to Harrogate every fortnight, in one of Wood's taxis, to Austin Reed's for a hair-cut. He always had the best of 'Hardy's' tackle, which he looked after as only a gentleman of leisure could. When he went fishing he would engage a Wood's taxi to take him to his chosen starting point and arrange where he was to be picked up for lunch. He always took off the cast, reeled in the line, put the reel in a chamois bag and the rod in the partitioned bag for each journey. Not for him, holding the rod out of the window or the sunshine roof! But of course, for him there was all the time in the world.

On one occasion he was bolder than usual and waded towards the deep pool below Ferryhouse where he shipped water into his waders, panicked and shouted for help. I went to his assistance and could have verbally guided him into shallow water and safety, but he was convinced that the water was rising rapidly and lost his nerve. I went in and rescued him and he insisted that I should accept a 9′3″ split-cane rod and a 'Hardy', 'L.R.H. Lightweight' reel worth in 1927 about £24, which included the Kingfisher line. Today, the rod and reel are as good as new and worth more than they were then. The rod is still as straight as a die and a pleasure to use, even though many anglers would consider it to have been superseded by other materials.

The only way locals could fish for trout was by being given a complimentary ticket from the Duke's Agent, although we were given a free ticket to fish for grayling during the Winter months and were allowed to use worm, while the trout fishing was strictly 'fly only'. The complimentary tickets were usually for evenings only or for a limited catch on a particular stretch of the river. A rough field called Lime Bottom was often allocated, which had two angry Ayrshire bulls tethered in it. At another period, herds of pigs roamed there living in 'Pigloos', with attendant, unpredictable boars! However it was worth running the gauntlet as this field was little used by the hotel residents.

One added spice was that some of the opposite bank was the preserve of the Bradford Waltonian's Club, so when we caught with a long cast, it was, as it were, 'stolen fruit'. In those days they had, unlike many clubs, started putting in a good stock fish. It was said, rightly or wrongly, that we were in order fishing past the half-way point, provided we waded in reverse to what could be considered our half. Following this advice I sat down in the water on an icy day and thereafter avoided this manoeuvre.

Continuing upstream from this point to Bolton Bridge is the length I have known best, being able to see much of it from Ferryhouse, where I have observed the river in all its moods. Hambleton Beck, which ran into the Wharfe a few hundred yards below the house, was a considerable feeder stream and acted as a nursery for smaller fish, but the only restocking was done by the 'Beck Watcher'. He stripped female fish in late Autumn and took the ova to a small hatchery in nearby Storiths, where there was a small building with three stone troughs, fed by a stream of piped water and each discharging into the lower one, like a salmon ladder. The fingerlings were returned to the feeder streams the next Spring.

In August, when King George the Fifth was staying at Bolton Hall, the river was very low and fish were hard to catch. The 'Beck Watcher' was unable to catch sufficient fish for the needs of the Hall kitchen, so on the flat, calm stretch below Bolton Bridge he decided to drag the water with a long net. This had cork floats and lead weights on the bottom. He and his son, both wearing chest-waders, pulled the net some hundred yards. The son crossed the river and they both pulled the net into the field. Several milk churns were filled with fish and many more undersized ones were returned to the water. The 'Beck Watcher' at that time was Joseph Hudson and his son Alan was a gamekeeper. Chest-waders were not used by anglers as the chances were that if they fell into this fast-flowing river the legs of the waders being full of air would buoy them up, with the fisherman's head under water. The permits of the day stated 'wading stockings only allowed'. This wording, which seemed archaic at the time, referred to the macintosh type thigh-length waders, which were worn with and protected by specially made brogues, which let the water in and out.

I was poaching one night in the pool below Ferryhouse and in an attempt to shrive myself I must admit I was worming, when vengeance descended from the night sky and put an end to such lapses, once and for all? I was standing on the bank, keeping absolutely still and quiet, just lifting the rod occasionally, when I sensed a presence at my right shoulder. I turned my head and was as startled as the heron which had planned to land just about where I was standing. The bird, huge at this range, had to gain height quickly to avoid colliding with the bridge and the noise made by its wing beats was unbelievable at such close quarters. Also, in its fright it made such awful screeching and worst of all it emptied its bowels all over me! When I partially recovered I decided that my only course was to clean myself up, by going into the river fully clothed: another salutary lesson on a cool, Summer night. In case anyone should have the idea of reporting me to the 'Beck Watcher' I claim immunity under the Statute of Limitations. I did in any case, years later, tell the riparian owner, the Duke of Devonshire and he was vastly amused.

Joseph Hudson, who was the 'Beck Watcher' for many years, 'dressed' beautiful, artificial flies and grew one thumb-nail to a long, sideways point to help with this job. He told me that on one occasion, towards dusk, when he was crossing the stepping stones near the Priory he saw a tremendous 'rise' of feeding fish. He took a stub of candle from his waistcoat pocket, lighted it and caught several specimens of the natural fly coming past. He walked home to Storiths, some half mile, 'dressed' the artificial flies to match the specimens, returned to the river with his rod and caught 38 good fish. How many he kept was not revealed.

Angling in such an area as this has always been a delight. If sport was poor there were the joys of plants, birds and animal life as well as the companionship of fellow anglers. Mallard were not as plentiful as now. Herons have always been comparatively rare and even more so, kingfishers, goosanders, crested grebes and dabchicks. All of them are predators on the angler's quarry to a greater or lesser degree, but perhaps with as much right to them as he.

Today there is a more limited range of sports available locally than there was in the Twenties and Thirties. Whilst angling continues to flourish as well as cricket, more recently a 'health club' and a ladies' rounders team, Bolton Abbey of the Twenties and Thirties had more to offer. There was a golf course, a cricket team and three tennis courts, there was also an enthusiastic football team. There were regular visits from the Harriers in pursuit of hares, which were much rarer than they are now and the otter hounds came regularly, twice a year, but their quarry seemed as elusive then as now. I have only, as I have mentioned, seen four in my life and one of those was dead. I, as a boy, did envy the huntsman's livery, which was a glorified game-keeper's outfit with green stockings and a red tab protruding from the fasteners under the knee and for the fact that they took to the water when going under bridges or when the banking was impassible with trees. My envy was due to the fact that I was not allowed to walk in the river wearing boots. Wellies, which had not then been thought of, would have solved the problem!

There were three tennis courts. The Beamsley Tennis Club had one court which was open for locals at low cost, another belonged to a family at Benthill, which their friends also used and the third court was at the Devonshire Arms, which was for the use of the proprietor's family and friends and occasionally for guests of the hotel. The tennis court at the Devonshire Arms and at the Bolton Abbey Tennis Club were professionally laid out with a pavilion and high netting fence, whereas the one at Benthill, was simply a mown area on a piece of pasture land with a net across, but it gave a lot of pleasure to the Ward family and their friends.The Devonshire Arms tennis pavilion, the Beamsley Tennis Club pavilion and the Golf house were all made out of ex-railway guard vans. These were brought from Skipton and lifted onto site by Arthur Green's timber wagon teams. The van at the Devonshire Arms was finally demolished by a deliberate fire, one bonfire night. I took part in this destruction. Unfortunately the mains electricity, which had been installed by the late Thirties, had not been switched off after use and when the insulation burned off the cables there was a free display of fireworks. As if to compensate, when the water pipes melted, the display was somewhat dampened.

The football team unfortunately had only a short and undistinguished career. My brother Jack noted in his diary of the period, 'bought a pair of football boots, price fourteen shillings'. Today the Devonshire Arms Hotel has its own staff football team, but there is not a football team at Bolton Abbey for locals. Boyle and Petyt School boys are encouraged to take an interest in football, so perhaps in the future such a team may be formed and flourish.

The golf course was laid out on Hospital Farm, the land behind the Alms Houses at Beamsley. The Club House was in a central position for the course. I t still exists but is now fairly derelict and known as 'Woodlands'. The proprietor did it all; he laid out the course, mowed the greens, provided a golf shop, which he staffed and acted as 'professional' and taught all who wanted tuition!. The course was fairly popular with some locals for a time, but the club ultimately died the death with the proprietor turning to other, more profit-making schemes, such as the Bolton Abbey Dancing Academy.

Mr George Douglas of Farfield Hall, President of the Bradford Dyers' Association, had shoots on his own Beamsley farms and woods, mainly pheasant, with the occasional covey of partridge, and he reared many birds. He also had the Devonshire Estate's pheasant shooting. The Head Keeper on the Farfield Estate, Mr Larkin, lived at Resphill, near Bolton Abbey and used the existing barns to house the hatching coops and pens; for in addition, he had dog kennels. For the keeper's convenience there was a boat provided to cross the Wharfe at the point still known as Boat Wood. This boat was attached to a wire rope and shortened the distance from Resphill to Farfield very considerably. After ascending the field past Paradise Laithe, a barn which is now a dwelling, the Addingham Road was crossed by a wooden footbridge, locally known as 'Wishing Bridge'. This became obsolete as the boat disappeared and the bridge was dismantled after being damaged by high loads on vehicles travelling on the road, long ago. Mr Larkin had two under- keepers, Benny Moorhouse and Alan Hudson while Douglas Tiffany, now living at Embsay near Skipton, was the apprentice. There were two cabins for their use in Struff Wood on the bank of the Wharfe and Westie Bank and each cabin had its sinister galleries of vermin in various stages of decay, to demonstrate that the keepers were doing their job. I have no record of the 'bags' shot by Mr Douglas, their employer, but I do know that they were considerable.

Hardly 'Sport' I know, but I thought you might be interested anyway! The Bolton Abbey Poultry Society used to stage an annual competitive Poultry Show, in which the ladies also vied with one another in their 'Bread and Cakes' section. Almost everyone in the district was a 'fancier' and jealously guarded their own pet breed of fowls. Their Leghorns, Wyandottes, Buff and Barred Rocks, Light Sussex, Old English Game Birds and many more would now be considered rare breeds. Today, Mr Eric Nelson of Storiths still breeds varieties of fowls which attract people from distant parts.

Chapter 16

The great advantage of a hotel is that it's a refuge from home life

'You Never Can Tell' Act 2: George Bernard Shaw

The Devonshire Arms Hotel, a 17th Century coaching inn, now called the Devonshire Arms Country House Hotel, appeared in the Twenties and Thirties to many local people, rather like a land-locked, luxury liner, which had nothing to do with them. Something of that feeling still exists, although more locals now use it. Some people were as unfamiliar with the inside as if it had been on the moon!.

My first memories of it are of when I went with my brother at Christmas to be presented to Mrs Fawcett, the wife of the proprietor, who said the traditional few words and gave us a pencil box or a kit of Harbutt's Plasticine and some sweets. The children of Mrs Fawcett's chauffeur, Bobby, Elsie and Billie Kemp were there and they were given a complete set of clothes from head to toe, with underwear. They also received sweetmeats and after the short ceremony, were dismissed.

Starting from the end nearest to the village, the first building on the road-side was for the engine and dynamo that made the electricity, stored upstairs on a specially reinforced floor in large, battery cells. Behind the engine house was the garage for Mrs Fawcett's Austin Twenty and later her Armstrong Siddely. This garage was heated by a small, solid fuel stove, built into the wall outside and feeding hot-water pipes. The point of putting the fire outside was twofold, it was less of a fire-hazard and the fire could be de-clinkered and made up without opening the doors and letting cold air in. The next building, now the 'Duke's Bar', with two wide doors to the road and similar doors opening onto a yard at the rear, was garaging for six cars and had obviously been used as a stable at an earlier period.

After a single garage to the road-side came the Refreshment Room, which the thousands of visitors who came by train frequented. Obviously the name, 'Refreshment Room' was one they were used to and which stood in railway language for tea-rooms, bar, etc. This room was very big and on its full-length bar there were about four sets of beer engines, a fire-place at each side and with pitch- pine screens to protect those having tea with children from seeing the bar. These were on wheels and rather like cricket sight-boards. Later they became part of a permanent dividing wall. The roof timbers were supported on stone corbels and there were large bolts to act as tie-bars. The single-storey room was very high and had no false roof and the underside of the slates were covered by varnished boarding. Later and in stages, a ceiling was put in, below the tie-bars, with a floor above them and the vast space filled with staff bedrooms. These were approached by an overhead passage and Woods made and fitted a fire-escape from this to the open passage below.

After this passage, which divided the old hotel from the extensions, there was a bare room with a table and wooden forms with an open fire in Winter and this was the Public Bar. In this room, customers waited patiently or impatiently. The impatient would bang the tables with their walking-sticks and shout to attract the attention of the reluctant barman/'boots', who, wearing the regulation sleeve-waistcoat and piped trousers, would eventually arrive and sullenly take the orders. He would walk on a passage, through the outer and general kitchen, along another passage, to a bar window in the wall of the General Office, returning with a loaded tray through the busy kitchen to his customers. He would then take their money and return to the General Office to pay and collect their change. The front of the building had a coal-hole with a chute onto the front corner. The coal was used to fuel the kitchen stoves. Next were the Pastry Pantry, two kitchens, one mainly for washing up, and the General Office, front door and vestibule and then, a better furnished room for a 'superior' bar.

At the other side of the building from all these were the Cold Store, Still Room and entrance to the vast wine cellars. The Dining Room and Long Lounge were a similar lay-out as now with the Dining Room having a good view of the river and Beamsley Beacon, a 1,000′ hill beyond. The last of the original building was a Sitting

Room at the back and toilets at the front. These rooms were divided from the Dining Room by a passage known as the 'Fisherman's Passage' where residents' rods stood in the rod-racks provided. There was a weighing machine and a fixed measure to settle arguments on the length of trout or grayling that the fishermen residents had caught. It was here they would leave their waders or brogues for 'Boots' to dry and for these residents the Water Bailiff would attend daily to advise and provide artificial flies which he had 'dressed'.

In the late Thirties the demand for a Cocktail bar was very cleverly met by taking over a corner of spare garden on the road-side, which was ingeniously enclosed and built, complete with a fine, oak bar with mirrored shelves for bottles. No beer pumps were provided for draught beer. The Billiard Room was also a later addition with bedrooms above and the resident's staircase from the Long Lounge had to be adapted for these bedrooms. Another staircase not specifically for residents led to staff bedrooms and the Linen Store. There was a landing here which had no light from outside but was ingeniously lighted by a 'lantern', a square tower that cut through a bathroom, a ceiling and a roof void to a sky-light in the roof. It was very effective in bright weather and was appreciated before the advent of electric light.

The Hotel Farm was across the road from the original frontage and consisted of two pastures and a meadow, perhaps fifty acres in all and a large kitchen garden. These supplied flowers, vegetables and milk, cream and eggs. Mrs Fawcett had the Beck dammed below Huffa Bridge, opposite to the hotel, to make a deeper pool where the residents fed the almost tame trout after dinner. The ground between this pool and the tennis court was set out as a trough garden with each trough filled with soil and colourful flowers grown. For some years Mrs Fawcett bought every stone trough she could find and this garden was strolled in after dinner by guests on balmy Summer evenings.

With the exception of the farm man, gardener, groom, two chauffeurs, buttons and barman, the entire staff, cooks, waitresses and office staff were female. Many of the staff were maiden ladies who had made the hotel their home and 'service' a way of life, all quiet and deferential. The waitresses, some elderly after years 'in service', dressed in black, with long dresses and starched, white aprons, lace caps and starched cuffs and only disturbed the quiet with their rustling. I really envied 'Buttons' in his pill-box hat, the sleeve waistcoat with the puffed out chest (was it padded?) and the scores of highly polished buttons down the front. He had epaulets, one of which held immaculately starched, white gloves. He had 'tin-whistle' trousers with an elastic band from the bottoms which went under the instep of his mirror-like boots, to keep his trousers taut. He also was given *half-crown* tips, had an 'Alldays and Onions' motor-cycle and . . . a girl-friend!

The rule about employing mainly female staff applied all the time that T.C. Fawcett and his wife had the hotel, from around the end of the First World War until 1939. (The Fawcetts had previously owned the Palmer Flatts Hotel at Aysgarth, North Yorkshire). The hotel has always been well-known and patronised. I cannot recall there ever having been a 'bad patch'. Why did people come? They probably came because it seemed to have had an enviable reputation as 'one of the finest country hotels in England', since it had superb cuisine and cellar, was elegantly and comfortably appointed, and had discreet service.

The over-riding atmosphere of the place was of quiet gentility and the luxurious, thick carpets and richly elegant curtains, furnishings and fittings together with hushed voices, all contributed to create this ambience. The fine, old building fitted comfortably into its surroundings in beautiful Wharfedale which the residents could view from the windows. During the Twenties and Thirties the hotel only had a 'Six Day Licence', which meant that non-residents could not get a drink on a Sunday and therefore the hotel was quiet and more attractive as a result. The luxurious hotel with attentive staff provided an extension to the homes of those resident at the time, who were used to receiving every attention and there was always an ample number of staff, with a good ratio of staff to guests.

For most of the period the residents arrived in enormous American cars, eight-cylinder 'Buicks', 'Ford Lincolns', 'Hupmobile' or the

French, 'Delage', driven by a chauffeur, doubling as valet, and the lady was mainly accompanied by a maid, or companion and they often stayed for months. The English cars some guests used were mainly 'Daimlers' and a few had 'Rolls Royces'. The Royalty of the period used 'Daimlers' and the gentry may have followed their lead. The cars were the best of their day, always big with a partition between the driver and the passengers. Mostly they were equipped with a telephone, or rather a speaking-tube, with a flexible, covered mouthpiece for the owner and an ear-piece near the driver's ear. Many of their cars had the let-down, fold-away seats, designed for children or for occasional use by over-flow passengers and invariably they had Bedford Cord upholstery in the passenger compartment with a leather seat for the driver. As more and more guests came by car for dinner, car-parking became difficult, since the only off-road space was the setts at the road-side, in front of the Refreshment Room. Cars were parked on the road against the front door and on the road-side opposite, often reaching from the bottom of Skipton Road to the Smithy, some two hundred yards.

One semi-permanent guest was Mr Frank Beverley, who was Recorder for Bradford. He used to be accompanied by his 'man', chauffeur/valet, Fred Winter. He had a magnificent 'Straight Eight, Sunbeam (8 cylinder, in-line engine) fore-runner in its classic design of the 'Rolls Royce Merlin', 12 in-line engine fitted to Spitfires. The 'Sunbeam' had a separate exhaust port for each cylinder and the polished port for each cylinder and the polished pipes emerged through the polished aluminium bonnet. With its deep-throated exhaust note it was well-worth standing about an hour to see and hear it set off. The open tourer with hood folded down in good weather with a separate tonneau for each seat was admired wherever it went. Mr Beverley and his brothers owned the whole of Halton East, near Skipton and farms and moorland on the perimeter of Beamsley Beacon.

The hotel has always attracted a wealth of influential and famous people. Karl Marx came and J.B. Priestley found he could work there undisturbed. Many famous politicians, actors and actresses found they could escape from the limelight for a while and be quiet.

Mr Arthur Green who owned the large, timber concern used the hotel so that all the staff in his house might take a holiday, then return to Spring- clean the house prior to his return. He would therefore stay at the hotel for a month while the house was closed. What luxury, to escape Spring-cleaning and live in alternative comfort and elegance until his own house was made spick and span, with his staff refreshed. Another couple came for a fortnight each year and I found out after a few years, when taking them by taxi to Grassington, that they spent many months on a journey which started at the South coast and followed the Spring as it moved North.

The thing all these people had in common was that they were so rich, like Mrs Picciotti, a lady with a large cheque book, who seldom used cash and there was no need for her to keep a close check on her finances. She said she never bothered to fill in the cheque counterfoil as it was too much trouble. The people who stayed at the hotel had accounts in stores they frequented so they had little use for cash, except for giving small tips. On the other hand most ordinary people of the period had to live frugally within their means and paid for everything in cash, since this was one way of keeping a close check on their finances, while insurance policies helped to make sure they could be buried decently and endowment policies provided occasional treats for the family.

The guests would soon settle into their routine of long breakfasts, reading their morning papers, sitting on the lawn or going for genteel walks, with the chauffeur following in the car at a discreet distance in case of tiredness or rain. The district abounded with every type of walk, river-side, woodland or higher ground, but most of the residents were mature and not given to vigorous pursuits. The days were spent in touring, with ample picnic baskets, supplied as required, or the ladies might visit the high-class shops in Harrogate or Leeds, whilst the men would make a day of it, having their hair cut, like Mr Reid, followed by a Turkish Bath and so on.

'Luncheon', not 'lunch'. was a long procedure of five or six courses, followed by a sleep in an easy chair by the men, whilst the ladies retired, for the same purpose no doubt! Mr Reid, the fisherman, had a good appetite and was always ready for the gong.

One lunchtime he was with his friend, Mr Hudson, another fisherman, and water-colourist. The gong went and he walked straight in as Mr Hudson did not seem so anxious to dine. He came back in a few minutes looking cross and when Hudson asked why he said, "Damme man, there's a wretched squeaker in the Dining Room, frightful nuisance!".

Mr Hudson was not deterred by a crying baby and went in for lunch, taking about an hour, during which the 'squeaker' prevented Mr Reid from going in. When Mr Hudson returned, Mr Reid was even more irate when he was taunted that all his favourite dishes had been served, only to be shattered by the untruthful news that his most favourite dishes were now 'off'. This was too much for Mr Reid with his 'Titanic' mentality, who simply could not believe that such a thing could happen. According to all reports he went on for some time muttering, "No jape!" and "Intolerable!", etc.

It is not clear whether these were directed at the baby, its parents or the management.

Afternoon Tea was a ritual with Yorkshire Tea-Cake, sandwiches, scones, jam and cream. Miss Lizzie Petyt, from Hazelwood nearby, was a descendent of one of the young men from there who founded the Petyt Charity. Miss Petyt who appeared to me as an impoverished gentlewoman, augmented her income by selling these fruit cakes and her famous sponge cakes to the Devonshire Arms for Luncheon and Afternoon tea. Tea was a leisurely affair and passed the time until the event of the day. . . Dinner. . . for which they dressed.

Their reputation for excellence in food was well deserved. Fish, an intermediate course, was always served on a large, pink sea-shell and the last course at Luncheon and at dinner was cake and Stilton. These cakes, officially referred to as 'light, luncheon cakes' were also made by Miss Lizzie Petyt and contained a light sprinkling of dried fruit. Each table had a whole or half-cake depending on the number of guests, for them to cut from and the whole Stilton, rich with Port and surrounded by a large napkin, was passed from table to table.

The Billiard Room was used for entertainment after dinner and when billiards lost its popularity in these circles, the table was removed and the room turned into a beautiful Resident's Lounge. In fine weather the men walked after dinner to the bridges over the Beck or the River Wharfe, to feed the trout. Meanwhile the ladies usually played 'Bridge'. Guests often met other guests they had become acquainted with in previous years and the place took on the atmosphere of a house-party.

Mr and Mrs T.C. Fawcett ran the hotel with great style, with the help of their family and a large staff. Of their children, Peggy, the youngest, Norah and the eldest daughter, Dorothea, all eventually moved away, as did their only son, Phil. He bought and enlarged the small, country pub at South Stainley, near Harrogate and lived their with his wife and family. T.C. as Mr Fawcett was known had served his trade, starting at the bottom. He had a great sense of fun and said when he started as a lad in the off-licence department of a Leeds pub that he had, about closing time, a woman who wanted to buy a bottle of wine and he recommended a bottle priced at a shilling. She asked every question about the wine, the vintage, the vineyard, etc., and her last question that proved too much was, "Is it good for the blood?"

T.C. replied, "I don't know, but it's b----- good for a shilling!".

T.C. was however a gentleman and respected by guests and staff during his time as proprietor of the Devonshire Arms.

For many years, especially during the quiet, Winter months, the hotel was almost entirely taken over by the family, relatives and friends for huge house-parties. They amused themselves according to the weather by snow-ball matches, skating on the river or fish-ponds, playing croquet or tennis and went in for all the latest fads, such as jumping up and down the road on 'pogo' sticks. One labour-intensive and pretty unsuccessful diversion for the family was gliding from the high ground in the Bridge field, towards the river. The launch took some time, the glider was fastened to the ground with one person set to run holding the wing-tip. Two teams of men stretched enormous lengths of elastic rope as far as they could and when the glider was released, it became airborne for a short distance and landed, usually damaging the undercarriage. They were no doubt inspired by Herr Kronfeld who at that time was making regular trips from the top of Beamsley Beacon to the top of Wharfedale and returning to the launch-point. Woods supplied goods and services to the hotel, as well as the Wood brothers and their wives being part of the Fawcett's wide circle of friends who tested out the new cocktail bar. Also on two occasions on Winter evenings, when the hotel was empty of guests, we had to pretend to be hungry and thirsty members of a wedding party as an excuse for a 'binge' and on the first occasion, to try out the new cocktail bar.

Mrs Fawcett occasionally had 'mad' ideas, one such providing almost my last memory of the family. She decided one Winter day that she would like to be driven to the recently opened 'New Cinema' in Ilkley, in the hotel Victoria, a four-seater carriage, with a high, separate seat for driver and groom. For reasons I cannot remember, she wanted 'one of the Wood boys' to drive and as usual, my Father had one 'to spare', on this occasion, me. I caught our horse, 'Dick', who had on his thick, Winter coat and had been rolling in mud. I went over him with the curry comb and brush getting mouthfuls of hair and soil and in desperation, finally used a paraffin rag to try to make him presentable and as a final touch, I did his hooves with Archangel Tar and polished the harness.

The chosen route was via Nessfield and on the long drag into the village, Mrs Fawcett became impatient and asked me to go faster. Dick, who was the kindest horse ever without any vices, was on the lazy side and in all fairness, perhaps a bit out of condition. I tried to get a bit more speed out of him vocally and by shaking the reins vigorously, which merely dislodged more loose hair, which blew into my mouth. When this was of no avail I cracked the whip in the air. To have whipped him would have been as unthinkable as whipping one's own Grandmother and Dick knew this.

Arriving at Ilkley, terrified that any friends might see me in the hotel's ill-fitting, almost mouldy, coachman's outfit, I was told by Mrs Fawcett to 'put up' at the Crescent Hotel and 'bait' (feed) the horse. I often wonder what the proprietor of that hotel would have said to my request, as those days were already past. However I was saved by a bright idea. I told Mrs Fawcett that it would be dark when the film finished and there were no lamps on the carriage and that I had better go back home and send the car for her. She immediately agreed to this scheme and as soon as I was out of sight, I removed the coat, even though it had started raining, picked up a load of friends at Bolton Abbey bus-stop and returned triumphantly home. I had notched up another 'first' in Father's scheme of things.

The hotel was noted for its excellent food and wine; everything was fresh, in the absence of deep-freezers, except for pickled or salted beef, salted fish, home-fed hams and bacon. Some bottled and canned provisions were kept, mainly for staff. Meat and provisions were delivered by tradespeople in Addingham, Ilkley or Skipton and wine merchants delivered regularly. 'John Smiths' was the sole supplier of beer and their best bitter is still remembered. All minerals were from Cantrell and Cochrane (some name) of Harrogate. Regular supplies of fresh fish, packed in ice-boxes came by train, direct from the ports, and blocks of ice in sacks came almost every day by train from the Leeds Ice and Storage Company, which was used for 'cold chests' and for making ice-cream. In addition to their hotel, the Fawcetts also catered for race-meetings at Ripon, Beverley, York and Stockton-on-Tees and my brother, Jack and I drove either Mr Fawcett, or a van with supplies, to these courses. As we had permits to let us into Tattersall's Enclosure we were able to rub shoulders with the best. Mr Thomas Craven Fawcett once said that catering for race-courses was a 'dead cert', if the punters had had a good day, they celebrated with oysters and champagne and on a bad day, they would drown their sorrows with the same mixture!

On one occasion my friend, George Demaine, and I had collected money and bought a wreath for the Duke of Devonshire's Agent, Mr Down's, funeral and due to late subscriptions we found ourselves with a surplus of three pounds. I wondered what was the correct way to dispose of the surplus and when talking to George about the subject he said, "Don't worry, I know what to do".

Later we had dinner at the Devonshire and toasted "Absent Friends", with money left over for the tip!

It was the end of an era of happy times and a friendly, business association when Mr and Mrs Fawcett had died and the family had handed over the hotel to the Hodgsons in 1939, although that was the beginning of another happy relationship. During the Fawcett's time the hotel had flourished and provided an orderly, elegant, luxurious and peaceful, temporary home for many thousands of guests and hospitality to many more. Meantime, Woods were well-established in the work they undertook at the Smithy, which had evolved according to the demand from the public, the Estate, local people and the Devonshire Arms Hotel.

TELEPHONE:
BOLTON ABBEY, 27.

CHATSWORTH ESTATES
COMPANY.

DIRECTORS:
THE DUKE OF DEVONSHIRE, K.G.
THE MARQUESS OF HARTINGTON.
U. ROLAND BURKE.
A. H. BATTCOCK.
R. J. F. BURROWS

ESTATE OFFICE,
BOLTON ABBEY,
SKIPTON.

7th. May 1935.

Dear Sir,

In reply to your letter and our interview on the 30th. ulto, I enclose letter transferring the Tenancy to your four Sons from Lady-day last, you paying the Rent due to that date.

I return the Insurance Policy and Receipt, also the Rating receipt, for which I thank you.

Yours faithfully,

E C Downs

Mr. Robert Wood,
BOLTON ABBEY.

Chapter 17

Under the Spreading Chestnut Tree the Village Smithy Stands

Henry Wadsworth Longfellow, 'The Village Blacksmith' (1839)

For all that my Father had been a tenant of 't'Duke's' at the Smithy and Ferryhouse with the land and outbuildings from Lady Day 1919, it was not until 1935 that the firm was officially formed, when Father retired to hand over to his four sons. In a letter addressed to my Father from Mr Alfred Downs, the Duke's Agent dated 7th May, 1935 the tenancy was transferred to three of my brothers and myself. The four names appeared very proudly on all the firm's stationery for many years, gaps only appearing as death took its toll, a truly family business. From the start of the business, progress was steady, but as cars became more popular, the repair and taxi side of the business flourished and that work increased as the shoeing side of the business, over time, became less in demand. In addition to our main smithy work Woods had many sidelines, some which were regular and some intermittent. One of the regular items we sold during the Twenties and Thirties was paraffin which was stocked and sold from a 50 gallon drum for heating and lighting. For many years a constantly recurring item on accounts was for cod-liver oil. We accidentally obtained a stock of this and then created a demand for its use in the district!

At about 2.30 am the driver of a wagon carrying barrels of cod-liver oil changed down into third gear near the Alms-Houses at Beamsley. The extra speed thus applied to the fly-wheel caused it to burst and fly apart, fragments of the metal being buried in the gate of Meadowcroft House, like pieces of shrapnel. As a result of this the driver had one leg injured, the brake fluid pipe was severed, making the foot brake useless and the main wiring harness was destroyed, putting out all the wagon's lights. The hapless driver driving by pale moonlight, slowed down as he approached the top of Mirk Hill (about 1 in 7 with a bend at the bottom at Bolton Bridge) only to gain speed as he went down the hill. On reaching Bolton Bridge he was unable to turn the corner and ran into the bridge wall. His load pushed forward into the cab, injuring the driver still further. The impact caused the barrels to fly through the air into the river, with each making a 'crump' as it landed. The force with which they hit the water caused such pressure inside the barrels that the brass, threaded bungs were forced out. These flew through the air whistling and shrieking like live ammunition and some were found a quarter of a mile from the scene. Next morning Father organised the family on a rescue operation and recovered so much oil that we had it on sale for years. He created the demand for it by saying how good it was for sickly cows and other animals, which did seem to benefit some of them, so it was bought for years for that purpose. During the weeks before the local Poultry Show many exhibitors bought it since, as Father had pointed out, it made the feathers shine and the combs full of colour. Little did it matter that the hen's eggs tasted of cod-liver oil for weeks!

To capitalise on the 'radio boom', Woods became agents for 'Brandes Radio' sets and installed many of these. My job was to erect the aerials, about 25 yards of copper wire, suspended between a convenient building or tree and the house chimney and insulated by white, 'egg' porcelain insulators. The lead into the house was effected by drilling a hole through the window frame and inserting a lead-in tube, made of insulating material, and with a brass middle bolt with terminals at each end, a wire from the inner one being plugged into the receiving set. Prior to the advent of valve wireless set it was only possible to receive signals and programmes on the 'crystal set' using ear-phones. This had to be in a perfectly quiet room. The most infuriating interference was from some person in the room turning over the sheets of a newspaper. The 'crystal set' consisted of a long tube of cardboard with wire wrapped round it over which the operator moved a larger and much shorter length of cardboard, also with a wire wrapped round it. The 'power' was provided by a piece of crystal, held firmly in a brass cup. This was probed to find the best facet by the 'cat's whisker', which was a short, springy wire held in a small rod with a universal ball-joint. This rod could be rotated in many directions and held secure when the best facet was found. In the early days of the valve set, most sets were made by amateurs and were remarkable contraptions of wires, valves, tuners, etc., still made from cardboard tubes. The power was supplied by a two volt accumulator which had to be re-charged about every two weeks, thus all Wood's till rolls had the entry, '2v. acc. chgd', countless times. Later, factory made 'radios' appeared, powered by dry batteries, 'high tensions ' and 'grid bias', a great improvement as the accumulators were filled with sulphuric acid, which, if spilled on clothes, car carpets or household fabrics burned a hole in them in a matter of hours.

In addition to our being 'Brandes Radio' agents another interesting sideline was provided by Stockholm Tar, which was sold from a wooden barrel with the top staved in and dispensed into the customer's own receptacle with a wooden device like a small cricket bat. Stockholm or Archangel Tar was used as a remedy for many cattle ills, from foot-rot to a salve for injuries, an example being lambs who had excessive bleeding from their tail stumps, after their tails had been shortened. The bleeding was first stopped by the application of a handful of cobwebs, then the tar was applied to the area. On special occasions horses had Stockholm Tar applied to their hooves, which coloured them black and 'finished off' their appearance. This was a quality which was especially useful to people who were particularly horse- proud, or who wanted a matched pair in every detail. Fred Nelson at Blubberhouses applied the tar every morning to the hooves of one of Mr Galloway's carriage horses at Blubberhouses Hall, since one of its hooves had a white streak.

Meanwhile, George, now joined by Jack, was shoeing horses, often eight a day at the start of hay-time and always making ironwork for gates for the Estate, a task which continued throughout the 57 years we were in business there. Thinking about this one day and trying to find something to occupy the children in the school taxi we ran, I asked them to count the gates on the roadside between Beamsley School and Bolton Bridge, about half a mile. I was amazed to find there were fifteen gates onto the road, which meant there were 105 items of Smithy-made fittings. So multiplying that by the number of gates on the Estate and allowing for corrosion by weather, occasional accidents, lack of oiling, etc., it was small wonder the fittings were always in demand.

At the instigation of Mr Downs, the Agent, we came to an agreement to have a common language for ironwork, so thus evolved for gates, 'crook to screw', 'crook to drive', 'loop to screw', 'gate-chains' and 'gate-chain hooks' and for doors, 'ring handle', 'latch', 'catch' and 'carrier'. There was also 'crook to lead-in' (to lead in with molten lead to a stone gate-post). This did away with such words as 'sneck', 'holdfast', 'tumbler', etc. Mr Romilly B.Craze, architect partner with Sir William Milner, bart., was overseeing the building and enlargement of Parceval Hall further up the Dale at about the same time and had the same exercise with the tradesmen on that job, to determine whether to call the roof timbers, 'purlins', 'joists' or whatever. He said that many of the names the local tradesmen used were of Scandinavian origin.

Many of the articles made by the blacksmith in the Smithy fire were so right for the job and a delight to see and handle, but as skilled men, generally, became more and more rare, many of the items were made by machinery but were poor, ugly imitations. The Wood's design for making the 'chain gate hook' was just right for the job and a relatively simple and effective way of fastening a gate. Most gates were fastened by a length of chain attached to the gate-head by a staple (preferably smithy -made) and the 'gate-chain hook' at the other end of the chain engaged with another staple driven into the gate-post. The design of Wood's patent 'chain hook' was that when all was correctly fitted it engaged so easily and prevented the gate 'napping' against the gate-post in a wind. 'Napping' in this context is a local, hybrid word, a cross between knocking and tapping and here is a slightly 'tongue-in- cheek' example of what could happen without a Wood's design of 'chain gate hook' being used.

One windy night for want of a Wood's 'gate chain hook', the farmyard gate napped each time there was an extra gust. Each time the gate napped, the dog barked and the farmer stirred in his sleep, tensed and listened. Each time he stirred, he disturbed his wife. By morning the farmer, usually a mild-tempered man, was so frayed that he snapped at his wife over breakfast, saying regrettable things which upset her so much that she was almost brought to tears. Their daughter went to her Mother's side and remonstrated with her Father, who turned his fury on her. The result? The daughter left home, lived in lodgings in a nearby town and worked in Woolworths. She started wearing silk stockings, high heels, lipstick and talking to boys. . . . the catalogue is endless. . . . and all for the want of a Wood's 'gate chain hook'!

In about 1924 we built a Dutch barn in the orchard to accommodate the extra hay grown as a result of intensive farming, the old hay-lofts being inadequate. We also cut and made hay on any suitable roadside verges and cut, made hay and carted away the grass from the Priory grave-yard, for which we paid the Parochial Church Council the sum of ten shillings. Also in the orchard we built a corrugated iron shed to house the waggonette and made a rack for stocks of bar iron, etc. In this period, before my brother Herbert joined us in the business, the work undertaken besides horse-shoeing and general repairs included making many sets of grappling irons. These were placed on a display board at the Strid with a life-belt and there were instructions for helping people who had fallen in, but unfortunately all these items were thrown into the water so often by vandals that it became useless to replace them. There was a constant demand for new 'horn burns' (branding irons) for horned sheep and for the re-cutting of letters on old ones. Jack was a specialist in making them and used to test them on the Smithy door, which is still there, now painted over, covered in initials.

Much heavy haulage was done by Sentinel steam wagons, which produced high charges of static electricity and as they were on solid, rubber tyres the charge could not return to earth. To remedy this they trailed a strong chain, rather like a later device to help passengers avoid car-sickness and as the chain wore away a new link had to be made, often by Woods, and fitted. When this work was neglected the static electricity charge from the iron steering wheel to the driver's wet hands was enough to knock him over. There were many entries to the firm's books in the late Twenties and early Thirties for repairs to the carbide lighting plant to the Village Institute and billiard table. The recurring job, then and during the whole of the firm's existence was the repairing, re-shafting and sharpening of tools, hay-rakes and such and rake teeth were also stocked as well as rake-bows, complete with heads and shafts.

Among those who came to work for us during this time were John Parkes of Ilkley, now living in Addingham, 'Pro' Nelson and Dick Sutton of Bolton Abbey, Jack Norris of Addingham and others who all made a contribution to the success of the business. Bert Ward of Bolton Abbey came to help us out for a week and stayed for 30 years! Bigger jobs were undertaken as we started to employ the extra staff, for example a fire escape was made and fitted by Woods at the Devonshire Arms when the overhead passage-way was built from the main part of the hotel to the new bedrooms over the Refreshment Room.

One fascinating item we were asked to provide was for chains which had to be coupled together to reach round one of the stone piers that carry the Stepping Stones Bridge, near the Priory. This pier had been moved over at the top by the bridge being battered by a high flood which eventually took most of the bridge away. This chain was then pulled by six of the mighty Clydesdales of Arthur Green's team of timber horses. The motor wagons of the day, even if they had the power would not have had the grip. It was an awe-inspiring sight to watch this spectacle of the combination of man and horse-power to restore the bridge.

One elegant item we made in 1926 was high, iron fencing for the kennel runs at Beamsley Hall to contain Mr Booth's pedigree mastiffs and these are still in place at the Hall. After making ornamental ironwork for Sir William Milner for Parceval Hall we had a long association with his firm of Milner and Craze, Architects, with offices in London. Wrought ('wrot') ironwork, mainly door furniture was made for St Alban's Church, Becontree; St Thomas's, Enfield; St Martin's, Hull; St Alban's, Hull and St Aidan's Church, Hull.

We made wrought iron door furnishings and vast quantities of hand-made nails for the Shrine of Our Lady of Walsingham. The first twelve seemed to take an eternity, after which it became easier. We also made a rather fine balustrade for the Shrine, which turned a corner for a second flight of stairs, a difficult manoeuvre in wrought iron-work. The newel post was beaten out of a piece of square metal to make the shape of a serpent's head. When this piece of metal was heated in the fire all six of our staff could hammer it with the big hammer, until they ran out of wind. Other wrought iron-work was undertaken for St John's Church, Coventry; St James', Pinner; All Saints, Queensbury; Holy Trinity, Bingley; Acomb Parish Church; the Parish Church at Withernsea and lych-gate fittings for the Church at Long Preston. We also made an elegant set of gates for the Editor of 'The Times', Geoffrey Dawson and light-fittings, curtain rods, and fittings for Bolton Priory.

The Post Office telephones were starting a programme of automating rural telephone exchanges. As a result of this our number had to be changed from Bolton Abbey 11 to Bolton Abbey 21. We got the contract for supplying a set of wrought iron-work for many of these rural exchanges. They were all identical in lay- out and varied only to meet the needs of the environment where they were to be placed. The building contained switch-gear and large, glass, storage batteries to power the system. These were retained after the advent of mains electricity as they were unaffected by power-cuts. There was also a small engine, dynamo and switchboard to re-charge the batteries. The petrol tank for the engine was outside the Exchange in a lockable, fixed container to reduce the risk of fire. A Rural Automatic Exchange set consisted of a foot-scraper, the lockable petrol-tank holder, a full set of gate-ironwork for the gate to the exchange plot, a complicated cable- carrier, like a dinosaur's vertebrae with side-shoots to carry the cables from one part to another and other small items.

In 1926 the telephone was installed, no doubt to get more business for our recently acquired taxi and cabriolet 'Ford Model T' and the 'phone was one of very few in the district. The others were at the Post Office, Estate Office, Devonshire Arms Hotel and at the 'big' houses. Thus most people needing to use a telephone came to Woods who were open all day, every day until late in the evening and sometimes all night: mind you most customers were also good friends. Some difficulties arose when distant callers asked us to deliver messages to their friends or relatives in the district. This often resulted in our having to ask the recipients for the taxi fare as we delivered the message in our own taxis. They were sometimes reluctant to do this as they also sometimes had to pay the 'phone charge for us to send the return message. Most of the people who came to us to make telephone calls for them could not use the 'phone, even if we put the connection through. This was time-consuming for us but we were seldom able to make the caller get over his dread of the machine. Thus, ringing up Bob's brother John in Leeds to arrange a funeral went something like this:

Me: *(On the 'phone to John)* "Is that John?"

John: "Yes"

Me: "I'm ringing for your brother Bob about the funeral".

John: "Oh, put him on".

Me: *(In an 'aside' to Bob):* "He says, 'Will you talk to him?'."

Bob: "No!"

Me: "What do you want me to tell him?"

Bob: "Tell John I've fixed the funeral for Thursday".

Me: *(On the phone to John)* "He says he's fixed the funeral for Thursday".

John: "What time?"

Me: *('aside'* to Bob) "He says, 'What time?'."

Bob: "What time, what?"

Me: "What time is the funeral" . . .etc., etc., covering wreaths, taxis, funeral tea and so on.

It was no small undertaking, *(to coin a phrase!).* I was so frustrated with a similar call that I said to the caller,

"For goodness sake talk to him, I can't waste any more time".

Eventually he was persuaded and took the telephone very tentatively and in a voice hoarse with emotion said the magic words,

"This is me!". After breaking the sound barrier and 'taking a giant step for mankind' he spoke in monosyllables till the one being called rang off. The caller was proud of his achievement and said, "By gum, I were fair capped wi' that. It sounded just like our John!".

At a time when the Post Office Telephones wanted more people to install the 'phone they had postage stamps franked with a suitable message. One of our 'telephone customers' arrived one day 'in a state' and said, "Whatever has happened Donald?"

I replied, "I don't know what you mean!".

He said, "Somebody wants me on the telephone" and produced the letter he had received by post with the stamps franked, 'You are wanted on the 'phone'!

One much-used service provided by Woods was the temporary storage of a multitude of things: anything from a 'spare lamb' for fostering, to a basket of fruit and vegetables and usually addressed, 'C/O Pink Cottage'. This was the old, former Toll House next door to the Smithy, where the bus stopped, but pulled down in 1941. Bus drivers simply used to drop these items off at the Smithy (The Devonshire Arms chauffeur lived there for a time and left the hotel in anger around 1939 after spraying the cottage walls with ink after which it was unoccupied). Occasionally these parcels got us into trouble as when a basket containing strawberries and green peas amongst other things, which were for someone we did not know who had taken rooms at a farmhouse. Many people who came into the Smithy took one of the strawberries or pea-pods thinking that one would not be missed! A few days later the owner came to enquire and seeing the obviously depleted basket and the floor covered with haulms and pea-pods remonstrated with us for not having delivered the parcel. When it was pointed out to him that that was nothing to do with us and that it was merely a public service without reward and a nuisance, he said, "You could have left them alone at least!".

In order to improve our 'service' and to save our time locating parcels, we made a wooden fitting with special provision for medicines left by the doctors and veterinary supplies. One day a farmer came in with acute indigestion and said,

"Has Dr Crabtree left me a bottle?" Looking in the cupboard he saw a bottle with his name on it and took it down and had a good 'swig', belched and said, "By gum that's wonderful stuff!"

It turned out it was a bottle of 'cow drench' from the vet. There was a bottle with his name on it from Dr Crabtree but he picked up the wrong one first. Even after he discovered his mistake he swore by the medicine and always used it from then on. The wooden fitting was well above the ground for safe-keeping of meat and other foodstuffs. George Fox, the Pork Butcher from Ilkley, and hawkers of foodstuffs called regularly and their customers telephoned their requirements to us. Foolishly, until we learned better, we paid for these items and got repaid without interest when the parcels were picked up. On one occasion a joint of beef was not collected and started to smell and although we had resisted starting a free delivery service we decided on this one occasion to do so. On delivering the meat, the housewife did not offer what we had paid to the supplier on her behalf and when our driver asked for the money (2/6) she said, "I'm not paying for that, it's not fit to eat!".

Apart from this occasion we had to start a small book-keeping system for these transactions to get our money back. The same man who made the purchases was not always on duty when they were collected. So prior to the 'system' the purchaser, any of the brothers or employees, had to tell the rest what had been paid for each item. They also had to inform us all when they noticed that such a parcel had gone, to ask whether the money had been paid into the cash drawer or the till, hoping that someone had taken the money for the goods. The 'system' at least meant we had a record of who owed what to whom!

So progress continued, Father being happy with his busy farm, conveying visitors in the waggonette and George doing the work required as a village blacksmith in a rural area with other members of the family expanding their skills within and outside the firm and Wood's taxi business, being the only one in the neighbourhood did well.

Chapter 18

If you can't leave in a taxi you can leave in a huff. If that's too soon you can leave in a minute and a huff

Bert Kalmer et al: 'Duck Soup' (1933) film; spoken by Groucho Marx

As few people had their own cars, the taxi trade flourished and as the demand for weddings, funerals, baptisms and so on increased, we bought our Ford Model T with the cabriolet body. On Friday nights cars were required for the dances in the district and, most Saturday nights, trips to the 'Pictures' in Ilkley or Skipton. We young drivers preferred funerals to weddings as the food was usually better and more plentiful, for most people were buried with ham and trifle! Often as the parlour was full of relatives in the regulation black and wearing hats, bowlers, or amazing 'confections' for the women, we were relegated to the pantry to help ourselves. Excuses were made to us for having to eat in this alfresco manner, quite needlessly, as we were not inhibited by this and were spared the tedium of thinking up pleasantries to exchange with our table partners.

My Father, meeting a train and taking a party of people to the Rectory in the cabriolet Model Ford, asked me to go and make sure that the gate to the Priory grounds was open (about a mile away) when he arrived there. I said I would go by bicycle but he said, "No. If you walk up you will be able to ride back".

He duly arrived, went down to the Rectory and drove back, straight past me. I ran up the hill to Bolton Abbey village, thinking he did not want to make a hill start. He was not there. After I had walked home seething, he just laughed and said, "I forgot thee!".

To the present day motorists, this episode will need some explanation. He would have been afraid to park on the slope. The Model T had poor brakes. Most drivers parking on a hill for some time would put a stone or a wooden 'scotch' under a wheel as soon as possible and Father would have been unable to do this or to have asked one of the party to do so if the gate had been shut. To explain further, the Model T had three foot pedals. The left one pressed down and held down engaged low gear, similarly the middle pedal engaged reverse and the right pedal was the foot-brake. A further complication, the hand-brake lever when fully forward allowed the car to engage top gear, after taking pressure off the low gear pedal. With the lever in the mid-way position the car was in neutral and the lever fully back operated the brakes of the rear wheels only.

The names of the cars of the period that we had make fascinating reading. A few are still in production. We had 'Austins', 'Rovers', 'Sunbeams', a 'Vauxhall', a 'Chrysler', a 'Morris', a 'Wolseley', also a 'Beans', a 'Crouch', one 'Hands', a 'Herbert' and a 'Clyno'. The most notable car we had was an Austin 10 (WW 7732), which cost £50, did 240,000 miles in our service without a major overhaul and was sold for £98. We also had a magnificent 'Hillman' saloon, eight-seater, perfect engine which would go in top gear at walking speed and, favourite of all, my own 'Austin Seven'.

The 'Austin Seven' had been owned by a Mrs Ellison of Leeds who shared a friend's house in Beamsley for the Summer months. She had a large family, four daughters and a son, all doctors of medicine in later life. The Austin Seven on which most of her family had learned to drive, some taught by me, was affectionately known as 'The Beetle' and its number YT 2821 is engraved on my heart. When Mrs Ellison was turned 70 and her family were not making such demands on 'The Beetle', she decided to learn to drive and under the wing of an extremely competent teacher, modesty prevents me from naming, she made rapid progress, amazing at that incredible age! She returned to Leeds for the Winter and I lost sight of her for some months until one day she phoned to say she had driven 'The Beetle' all the way to Scarborough to stay with one of her daughters and back, merely grazing her own gate-post on the return trip. She was so thrilled that she had bought a brand- new 'Austin Ruby' saloon and had taxed and insured 'The Beetle' for one year and would I go to her house and collect it as a present for my many kindnesses. Would I go? You bet I did!

Being young and full of enthusiasm, I really went to town on that car, rubbing it down with sand-paper and brush-painting it 'racing green'. I dispensed with the bonnet fasteners and replaced them with a thick, new, leather strap. I fixed a shortened steering joint on the propeller-shaft tunnel, amidships, between the seats, with a rod to operate the cut-off gear change, and replaced the bicycle-like tyres and wheels with small wheels and enormous balloon tyres. In common with most such models the two bearing crankshaft meant that the performance could only be 'hotted-up' to a limited degree, especially when the main bearings were worn and as, so often happened with continual hard driving and revving, the crankshaft broke. This was a blessing in disguise as it coincided with our early days in the garage trade and I was able to renew the crankshaft with new bearings. At the same time the engine was re-bored by Hepworth and Grandage of Bradford to the maximum oversize, thus increasing the capacity and I never tired of telling admirers, after I had memorised it, that it was fitted with 'Nelson bohnalite, split-skirt, invarstrut pistons'.

Mrs Picciotti, the regular, wealthy guest from the Devonshire Arms, asked me to drive her to Laund House for the far-famed afternoon tea supplied by the Misses Young. (Beatrix Potter once stayed at Laund House for a short holiday). I could quite well have driven her there and picked her up at a later time, but this did not fit her plans. She took the (not unattractive) office girl and 'match-maker' as she was, she told me to take was it Gloria? for a walk in the woods and rejoin her for tea in an hour. What blissful, lotus-eating days, looking for an early-flowering Geranium Pheum or the nest of a Pied Fly-catcher (much to the astonishment of Gloria, an adjectiveless, 'towny' girl); lying on the lawn waiting for tea, without a cloud in the sky and with the war-clouds gone in the 'War to end Wars' never to return?

One date to be looked forward to was the annual trip with Henry Croft and his wife and daughter to his wife's parents for fruit-picking and eating, in a well-stocked orchard and garden. On such trips as these we were always treated as one of the family. We were hired also of course for sight-seeing tours. I took Miss Townson, the teacher from the Boyle and Petyt school, with her house-keeper and companion, Miss Steele, and two other friends, a Mrs Steele and

Miss Fanny Breare of Addingham, on a tour of Scotland. The tour was for two weeks and covered Bamburgh, Edinburgh, Killin, St Mary's Loch and a stay on the border on the way back. The ladies invited me to share in their lunch-time picnic or meal, but I found my own accommodation. The charge for this trip was £24 which covered two weeks' use of an Austin 16 (Reg. KY 242), petrol, wear and tear, garaging (cars were never left outside at that time), my accommodation and wages!

When but a callow youth I took a fare from the Devonshire Arms to the Dorchester in London, an American lady with two abominably spoiled children. As was common practice, the doors of the car were hinged at the back and if they were opened accidentally while the car was moving, they swung out and back, breaking the check straps and usually the door handle buried itself, where it hit the body. Even worse, if this happened on a narrow road, the wide doors were in the way of other road users. I was 'on tenterhooks' the whole way that this might happen and was relieved to arrive safely at the Dorchester after being lost for miles and passing the entrance to the Zoological Gardens a few times. I stayed in lodgings run by a retired servant from Chatsworth House, which had been recommended to me. I took the opportunity to go to the Motor Show and saw the new 'Ford Eight', far beyond my pocket at £124 on the road!

A much more peaceful journey was taking a coffin, complete with female corpse, from Addingham to Cheltenham. The deceased's relatives felt they could not afford a motor hearse. Woods once more came to the rescue, saving the deceased from a burial in a place other than she would have wished, by their policy of trying very hard not to turn down any offer of a chance to earn an honest shilling! For this journey the front seat of the Austin 16 was removed and the undertaker made a miniature trestle, which was placed in the foot-well of the rear passenger area to stop the coffin rocking on the transverse tunnel. I used this small trestle for a foot-rest under my office desk for many years.

Mrs Willy Hartley, a kindly lady who attended every local funeral, gave me advice which I have not always followed. Before most funerals, in the days when many corpses were kept in the front room of the house until buried, the undertaker would say to the mourners, "Would you like to see him/her before I put the lid on?".

Many people mainly young ones gave the stock answer, "I would rather remember them as they were".

Not so Mrs Hartley. She said to me that if she viewed the body she would always know that the person had died and never make that awful gaffe, "How is your Mother these days?" when the person had died years before.

A 'marathon' I did on my own was to take Mrs Roberts and her servant from Farfield House to live with her niece in Forest Row, near East Grinstead. Mrs Roberts had been crippled with some Rheumatic complaint for about ten years and had not been downstairs for several years and naturally she was anxious to drive slowly through Addingham and Ilkley and other towns and villages on the route, with many diversions to particular points. Despite an early start, we were only about Bawtry at lunch-time, when we partook of a feast from a Fortnum and Mason type hamper, Mrs Roberts suggesting that I had a sleep after this. Having been confined to one room for years the journey must have seemed an enormous distance to her and she was surprised when I said that we had only covered about a quarter of the journey. The car I was driving was cooled by a water pump assisted by a radiator fan, but unfortunately it had had a bump in which the fan assembly had been rendered useless. As a consequence of this it was too hot to start after tea, in the 'pancake race' town of Olby, and I had to have a tow to start. After this I was terrified of the engine stopping at traffic lights and I had, where possible, to arrive when they were at green, or where this was not possible, to brake with the hand-brake to make sure the engine kept revving.

However, after a nerve-racking journey, we arrived somewhere near our destination at about 11pm. The only place that had a light on was a public house, so leaving the car on a convenient hill, I set off to ask directions, noting through a chink in the curtains the men in the pub still drinking after hours. I knocked repeatedly on the door, in my desperation knocking louder and louder, and eventually, after many noises of locks clicking and bolts being withdrawn, a tough-looking man with a shillelagh, the handle in one hand and the 'business end' in the palm of the other; asked me, what I wanted, knocking up law-abiding citizens at that time of night. Fortunately he knew the house I wanted which was quite near. Mrs Robert's niece had switched the outside light on for our benefit and this had attracted the largest flying insects I have ever seen, by the hundred. As we lifted out this tired, heavy lady, who was terrified that we might drop her, these insects bombed us repeatedly, without our having a spare hand to defend ourselves. My room had been booked at an Hotel in the nearby town, where a reluctant member of staff, who had waited up for me, gave me a meagre supper and showed me through the apparently ill-lit building to my bedroom. Maybe as a result of being over-tired I was unable to sleep in the 'spooky' room and being unable to lock the door I moved furniture against it and slept fitfully. Premonition? Some weeks later the papers were full of a particularly grisly crime in that hotel.

Taking members of the cricket team to Halifax in a 'Chrysler' fitted with the 'newfangled' fluid brakes, I was horrified when there was no response from the brake pedal. However many times I pumped it I was only able to use the gears and the transmission hand-brake, which stank and smoked after quite a short application. The car was fitted with an exhaust cut-out operated by a ring in the floor and when this was pulled the exhaust by-passed the silencers which made the most appalling din and as was to be expected, my passengers made full use of it, being oblivious to the peril they were in. Arriving, miraculously without trouble, I examined the brake-fluid tank, which was of course empty of brake-fluid. None was available and having been told that a mixture of castor oil and methylated spirits would do I set off on foot to get these items. After walking miles round the town I got supplies, filled the tank and not knowing the process of 'bleeding' I pumped the pedal up and down for hours. Eventually I managed to get about half a pedal on the second application. This was better than nothing, although it was nerve-racking when the first push had no effect and it was contrary to all impulses to let the brake off for a second go!

The corrugated shed in the orchard was increased to twice the size and the extension had a pit for examination and working on cars. Hambleton Beck was troublesome and often flooded this shed, causing much disruption and damage, first flooding the pit, then the garage, but this problem was never able to be resolved. Of course, originally we had been involved in repairing and maintaining carriages, carts and other forms of transport and when Herbert joined us he started working on the car repair and maintenance side of the business. Working all night to repair a car was a commonplace affair, either to catch up with promises given or for important clients who could not do without their vehicles. For example, according to our records, we worked all night to dismantle a car belonging to George Booth of Beamsley Hall for re-boring. Certain parts were difficult to obtain for some, especially foreign, cars and we often called on the tin-smith in Addingham to encase rusted silencers in a new skin of sheet-iron with genuine tin-smith joints, not having a welder in the firm at that time.

Hard times were reflected in the fact that people sometimes left their cars in lieu of train-fares home, as in the case of three girls who gave us their car, not having the money for repairs. One car we subsequently used for taxi work we obtained in this way. The owner had broken down on his return from holiday and had to be at work the next day or face 'the sack', so we accepted the car for the price of two and a half railway tickets to Newcastle and stood the cost of the new axle-shaft. We used this car to take the Langbar and Nessfield children to the Addingham school when the suspension bridge at Addingham was washed away by a flood in 1935 until the bridge was rebuilt. Luggage, spare wheels and watches were items left as surety that people would pay the car repair bill and sometimes these were not collected; for example the luggage filled with women's underwear samples which after two years were distributed round the womenfolk in the family. This led to my requesting a solicitor to draw up a legal document to regularise these exchanges.

In 1924, the year of the Wembley Exhibition, we installed our hand-operated petrol pump with a 500 gallon underground tank. The hole for the tank was excavated by our own labour. The sides were shuttered and concreted and the cradles formed for the circular tank to sit on. Gravel was brought from the checkstone bed (pebbles or cobbles found in bends in a river) opposite the Tithe Barn near the Priory. It was carried using our own horse and cart and riddled by hand to separate the sand from the gravel. as required. The tank was lowered into the hole by a wooden pole 'three legs'. All these operations, apart from the screwed pipe work, were performed by our own hands. The spare soil from the tank-pit was taken away by wheelbarrow as I have mentioned briefly earlier and built to form a not very effective flood barrier against Hambleton Beck flooding the buildings. In 1932 the Estate built a permanent garage, which made a great difference in many ways: the entrance to the new building meant the removal of the old scrap-heap and midden, jointly for the shoeing shed and our stable. It covered the ground formerly used for pig-houses, stable and coach house as well as much of the orchard. The new building was ingeniously 'married' to the Smithy and farm buildings with flat roofs and gutterings.

Many of the local families eventually had quite sophisticated electicity generating and storage plants, beautifully built with direct drive to the dynamo and polished, slate switchboards and in another room the large, glass, storage batteries. One such that we maintained was the three cylinder 'Pelapone', made in Wakefield, installed at Beamsley Hall. Oakfield House, Lowfield House and Farfield Hall all had similar models. We installed a less sophisticated plant at the Smithy, wired the buildings and did a similar installation at Newhall Farm at Beamsley. This early improvement meant the installation of an engine to provide electric light for the buildings and Smithy and the facility to re-charge batteries for the increasingly popular wireless sets, the valve sets by then having replaced the crystal 'cat's whisker' set. The engine had for some time pumped water at Newhall Farm and had been made redundant by the installation of a 'ram'. It was an American 'Chore-Boy' with a transfer logo showing a happy, young black boy with a big hat, doing the farm chores.

Further advances were brought about by the acquisition of a treadle-operated lathe, bought from a house in Ilkley and brought by me from the attic of that house on the four-wheeled rulley pulled by 'Dick'. The lathe was later operated by a 'Petter' paraffin engine. This engine on a calm day made smoke-rings all the time, these becoming bigger as they got further away and constantly being replaced by smaller ones, to the delight of generations of children, of all ages, who put their fingers through them. More equipment installed included a ten-foot high 'pillar-drill' which was a three-speed model and capable of drilling all day, doing anything from a ¼″ hole to 2″. Like all our petrol-selling competitors we advertised 'Free Air'. Why 'free' I wonder as most people availed themselves of this service and doing this at first with a hand-pump and then with a foot-pump became rather tedious and time-consuming, so we bought an air-compressor.

Another useful addition was a thread-screwing machine, which made it possible to make for example a bolt used in the manufacture of a wooden wheelbarrow, not stocked by anyone and measuring 20″ x 5/16th". At the other end of the scale it was possible to make a bolt to stop a building bulging, say 35′ x 1″ or even longer, by the blacksmith forming two loops on the end of as many full bars of metal as required, thus making a folding bolt of any length. On one occasion we had a call from the Estate to supply a large number of bolts for the Cavendish Pavilion Bridge. These I think were about 18″ x 1″ and we got in touch with several bolt suppliers without success. One bolt merchant said, "The only way to get those made is to find a country blacksmith with a threading machine who is strong in the back and weak in the head!".

We minimised the hard labour by sawing the metal to full length after threading. The other end was turned according to the thread required and was turned slightly below full-size. A full thread being made by the fact that the dies made the thread by cutting a continuous groove, the metal disturbed being pushed up to form the top of the thread.

A typical week's account for work done around the late Twenties was as follows:

T.C.Fawcett, Devonshire Arms Hotel.

One shoe removed: 1/8d *(this involved removing a horse-shoe,*

trimming the hoof and nailing the shoe on again).
Chopper, ground and sharpened: 9d.
Tin, black enamel: 9d.
Pony trap repaired: 7/6d *(A big job).*
Bucket soldered: 8d.
Repairs to harness: 8d.
2 Gallons of Paraffin: 2/4d.
6 Pigs ringed: *(noses).*
1 lb Sal. Ammoniac tabs.: 10d. *(for Le Clanche cells which supplied the power for ringing the bells in the hotel).*
Chandelier repaired: 2/3d.
Repairs to Billiard Room wireless: 7/6d.
Laying hedge: at 3/3d.

How does one sum up 'Woods', recently referred to by a local person as "something rather wonderful that happened to Middle Wharfedale"? A farmer customer who moved too far away for us to see to his needs wrote, 'Oh that Woods had moved with me. I have a very helpful, local engineer who does his best, but nothing can replace the marvels produced in the Smithy fire'. The success was due, I think, in part to our being a big and happy family; all but the eldest son, Herbert, who had been blighted by living through the 'depression' on Tyneside. Each one of the family, apart from Herbert, had our own special friends of our own age group which enriched life for us all.

Herbert's wife was a Nidderdale girl, Lily. Harry married Beatrice, the daughter of an Estate mason, and George married Rosamund, the daughter of the Estate 'Beck Watcher'. Jack married Annie, an Addingham girl, and I married Joyce from Ilkley. So even the 'extended' family came from a radius of about ten miles as the crow flies.

The Smithy was an 'institution' and a warm, fascinating place, full of interest and activity. The place was always busy with members of the family and with the two or three local people who worked for us. It was a great place to keep warm when the Smithy fire was roaring and to pick up the local news and gossip, to discuss the 'affairs of

State', to seek advice or not of course. Each of the family gave help and advice when it was asked for, on a wide variety of topics, from guidance about the progress of a relationship, to legal advice, which I was able to help with, having studied the subject, to an extent. I gave help on several occasions to those who wanted to make a will, with special attention to the fairness of distribution to children of large families, which were then the rule rather than the exception. There were many requests for me to write important letters and fill in difficult forms or insurance claims, etc. and I was once referred to at a meeting when a secretary was wanted as, "Thee wit' pen at back o' thee lug" and served on nearly all the local committees. One apparent 'good work' Woods did for the Parish was to build a bicycle rack for 12 cycles in the shed in the yard at the Smithy. I suppose that this was more for our benefit than the owners of the bicycles. Many people came by bicycle from around the area to catch the bus to Skipton and Ilkley and most came at the last minute, dropped their mounts and ran. This meant that to restore order out of chaos around the premises, someone had to pick them all up and stack them tidily. After the racks were made, all cyclists were told to use them or park elsewhere!

On one Winter's evening, the Smithy fire was glowing and the local policeman, 'Bobby' Smith, called. He had rather a fine voice and rather 'fancied' himself as a tenor. It so happened that one of the items waiting in the Smithy to be collected was a harmonium keyboard, which George set up on two oil drums and started to play, with me supplying the wind with a vacuum cleaner! Harry, who was an excellent baritone, the policeman, George and I started singing songs from Gilbert and Sullivan's light operas. The 'bobby sang tenor, Harry sang 'contralto', I sang 'treble' and George sang bass as a quartet. One beautiful song we sang was 'Strange Adventure', from 'Yeoman of the Guard'. The 'bobby' was in the middle of singing a solo, 'Take a Pair of Sparkling Eyes', with his cloak flung back over his shoulders, when the door of the Smithy opened and the sergeant walked in. He had apparently been waiting outside for the policeman to 'make a point' with him but decided to follow the sound and come in. He took in the scene and said, "I'd always suspected that you were all a bit mad, but now I'm sure!"

So the business prospered, not particularly financially, although we were generally solvent, but so far as being useful to the community at the same time as leading a happy life. The last job we started in the period between the wars was making vast quantities of mule shoes in readiness for the expected conflagration of war and this work continued for a number of years after the late Thirties for our troops in Burma, but that is another story.